Sex IN YOUR GARDEN

by

Angela Overy

Fulcrum Publishing, Golden, Colorado

Library of Congress Cataloging-in-Publication Data

Overy, Angela.
        Sex in your garden / by Angela Overy.
                p.   cm.
        Includes bibliographical references (p. 114) and index.
        ISBN 1-55591-335-0 (pbk.)
        1. Plants, Sex in. 2. Plants–Reproduction. 3. Flowers.
    4. Flower gardening. I. Title.
        QK827.094   1997
        582.13'0416–dc20   96-42380
                            CIP

Printed in Korea by Sung In Printing Company

0 9 8 7 6 5 4 3 2 1

Fulcrum Publishing
350 Indiana Street, Suite 350
Golden, Colorado 80401-5093 USA
(800) 992-2908 • (303) 277-1623

For all the Overys worldwide.

Top: *Field of Iceland poppies*
Cover: *Dianthus 'Coral Charm,' Kurt Reynolds, Goldsmith Seeds*
Title page: *Lily, Rob Proctor*

CONTENTS

1 ALL ABOUT SEX **7**
  Male Parts 11
  Female Parts 14
  Other Flower Parts 18

2 SEXUAL ORIENTATION **20**
  How to Avoid Incest 21
  Bisexual Flowers 22
  Making It Impossible 23

3 THE ULTIMATE ADVERTISING CAMPAIGN **26**
  How to Attract Attention in a Competitive Field 28
  Advertising with Color 30
    Flower colors that pollinators prefer 31
    How plants make different flower colors 32
    Changing color after sex 37
  Advertising with Scents 38
  Advertising with Shapes 40
  Landing Platforms 44
  The Age-Old Question 46
  Hairy Flowers 52
  Making the Size Fit the Client 54
  Composites 57
  Sex Through the Seasons 60

4 GREAT BRIBES **64**
  Nectar 66
  Pollen 68
  Other Rewards 70

5 PAIN AND SHAME   **72**

     Eating the Victims   74

     Murder Most Foul   74

     Fraudulent Advertisers and Pseudo-Copulation   76

6 INTIMATE PARTNERS   **78**

     Bees Do It   78

     Bumblebees: Bumbling Sex   82

     Wasps: Getting Waspish   85

     Butterflies: Fluttering About   86

     Moths: Enchanted Evenings   90

     Flies: Scraping the Bottom of the Market   92

     Beetles: Old Reliables   94

     Ants: Potential Pain   95

     Sex Is for the Birds   96

     Bats: Sex in the Dark   101

7 BLOWN AWAY BY THE WIND   **102**

     How They Do It   103

     Having It Both Ways   104

8 HUMAN INTERVENTION   **106**

9 FAREWELL TO THE FAMILY   **112**

FURTHER READING   **114**

INDEX   **115**

A BOUQUET OF THANKS   **120**

1 ALL ABOUT SEX

Gardening is fun. Growing plants gives people a feeling of connectedness with the rhythms of life. The smells of the earth and flowers provide both solace and exhilaration. The aching sweetness and sadness of autumn, the intense excitement and vitality that signs of spring awaken, even the frustrations of capricious weather and hard-to-learn plant names, are familiar sensations to a gardener. There is another more visceral pleasure, studied by botanists and plantsmen for years, but not widely understood. Whether you are a prurient or puritanical gardener, or just an observer of flowers, you know that flowers are the reproductive organs of plants. What you may only hear whispered over the garden fence is that plants need sexual partners, and their striving to attract them can be compared with human courtship.

Suppose you live in a world where you have to be bigger or more beautiful than your neighbor to attract a mate, where rivals offer free parking and fast food to their lovers and disreputable opportunists offer nothing at all, but lure partners with false promises and murder them. Imagine that your paramour lives across the street but you cannot get together, so you pay an intermediary. What if you wanted desperately to have children but possible partners had been killed or lived too far away? As a last resort you fertilize yourself.

Imagine being male or female for a while and then switching to the other sex? This may all sound like supermarket tabloid sensationalism but it happens every day. It is the sex in your garden.

Plants can't think like humans, but they do have male and female organs somewhat similar to ours, and share some of the same urgencies. Unlike most people, however, plants have no ethics and may use bribery, treachery or traps to help them succeed in reproducing. While human sex involves a range of activities related to human reproduction and gratification, and there are many different ways for humans to leave a legacy to this world, plants have just one goal—to produce seeds that will grow into the next generation.

Most animals rove around, select a mate, then grope about so they fit together and a sexual transfer can take place. Because plants are usually rooted in the ground they have to get something else to perform their sex for them, an accomplice that will carry the male sperm fast and accurately from one plant to the female parts on another.

Humans and other animals spend a good deal of energy trying to attract a mate.

Flowering plants' efforts are geared toward courting what are called pollinators, usually insects, then bribing them with food, shelter or other inducements to feed or poke about the plants' sexual parts and then go off to visit a similar flower. It is such a complicated and expensive mission that some plants don't bother to advertise at all and just expose their sexual glands to the wind and let chance take over. Other plants go to endless trouble to lure particular insects, birds or mammals, and it is the infinite variety of pollinators that cause the flowers we see in our gardens to look so diverse. This is the reason why flowers are different colors, sizes and shapes, why they have various scents and open and close at different times of the year or day. To accommodate all the world's pollinators, from the most selective insect to the most undiscriminating slug, the sex life of flowers is more varied than ever before, and more ingenious than most humans imagine. While both casual gardeners and owners of tastefully planned and well-groomed gardens are innocently enjoying their flower beds, the plants and pollinators are involved in a voluptuous and lascivious display of gluttony and fornication.

Natural Selection

The reproductive organs of a pine are pollinated by the wind.

Tree fern in southern New Zealand. Wind and water help ferns reproduce.

Flowers are a modern invention. Fossil records show that 250 million years ago there were many plants but no flowers. Ancient spore and cone-bearing plants, like ferns and pines, reproduced with the help of wind and water, just like their modern descendants do. Cone bearers are called *gymnosperms*. *Gym* means naked in Greek, and these plants have their sexual organs and seeds out in the open with no showy flowers. Scientists disagree on whether insects or flowers evolved first, or if they evolved together, but it is clear that it took a long time for a new order of plants, called *angiosperms*, to appear. This process may have started with a few leaves oozing sticky excess carbohydrates that insects found delicious. Gradually bunches of leaves around the plant's sexual organs evolved with enough appealing color and food to lure insects. These were the first flowers, often simple bowl shapes with leaflike petals. The male organs were exposed, but the female ovaries and seeds were hidden away for protection from weather and predators. Sometimes primitive beetles crawled hungrily over these plants, munching on them and accidentally transferring male pollen to the female parts, while early bees and wasps flew in to feed at the flowers, offering a more dependable sexual transfer than wind or water.

The flowering angiosperms have branched into thousands of brilliantly different varieties that have constantly adapted to new insects and situations. While this was happening, some flying insects, like bees, butterflies and moths, grew to rely on the flowers for nourishment, and they specialized, growing such features as extra-long tongues to reach the food and meshing their life cycles to match those of the plants suited to them. When these insects feed at flowers they have no idea of the sexual favors they are performing for the plant, but the codependency is so complete that neither can live without the other.

Magnolias are ancient flowering plants that have persevered; some are still pollinated by beetles.

9

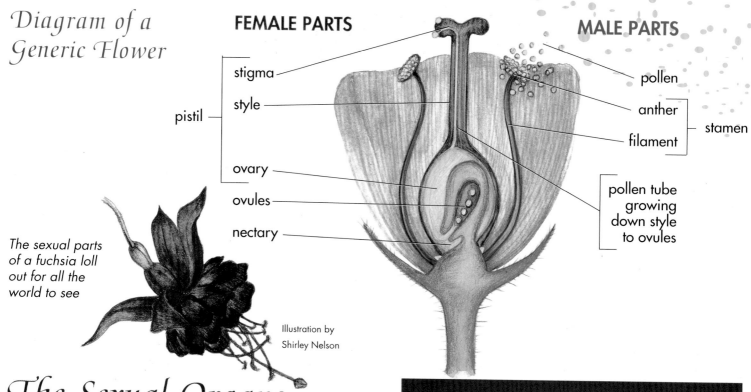

Diagram of a Generic Flower

FEMALE PARTS

MALE PARTS

pistil

stigma

style

ovary

ovules

nectary

pollen

anther

filament

stamen

pollen tube growing down style to ovules

The sexual parts of a fuchsia loll out for all the world to see

Illustration by
Shirley Nelson

The Sexual Organs

The sexual parts of flowers are not so different from those of our own bodies. Male sperm needs to transfer to the female receptacle in order for fertilization to take place. The male organs are on the outside for easy access. Female orifices are also on the outside while the ovaries are hidden, nurturing the offspring until they are sufficiently developed to leave the parent. While human sexual parts are much the same all over the world, those of plants are astonishingly varied. With apologies to botanists who may shudder at some of the terms, these are some of the basics:

MALE PARTS

STAMENS are the male parts of a flower. They often look like a bunch of little stalks in the middle of the blossom. The word stamen is easy to remember and refers to one male unit. In fuchsias the stamens are so long—sometimes two inches—that they loll out of the flower exposed for all to see. More reserved plants have short stamens tucked down inside the flower, or just stubs. Most are somewhere in between, dispensing pollen as they extend and shrink throughout the life of the flower. Different families of plants often have the same number of stamens in each flower, such as one for most orchids, five for campanulas or six for lilies. Roses and poppies have stamens in great whorls. All or some of a flower's stamens may be sterile; for example, penstemon blooms have four fertile stamens and one sterile one. Each stamen is almost always separate, but in some plants they are linked together to form a collar in the center of the flower around the female parts. Stamens consist of a stem called a filament. At the top is a purselike sac called an anther that is full of male sperm called pollen.

FILAMENTS are the stalks that hold out the pollen. They are often slender, springy stems that can bend and move as the flower matures.

ANTHERS are attached at the tip of the filament. Some are articulated about the point so they adjust to an incoming pollinator with maximum contact. Anthers can be seen easily on a large lily where they are smooth skinned when the flower first opens, then turn inside-out revealing the pollen. Anther sacs are often yellow but can be any color. Bright colored houseplant geraniums (Pelargoniums), for instance, have pink or purple sacs that can be seen scattered under the flowers as they wither. Anther sacs come in many shapes and vary a good deal in the details of the pollen dispersal. Some split open like a peanut displaying pollen, while others are spherical containers with little doors, flaps or valves to sprinkle pollen. Still others fling pollen out vigorously as they twist.

Stamens come in many shapes, sizes and colors.

11

Pollen Grains

Pollen grains are vehicles for the male genes of a plant. These complex, self-contained units have a life of their own and are so tiny that they usually look like yellow or orange colored dust. Most plants produce masses of pollen. Corn produces about 25,000 pollen grains to fertilize one corn kernel. This may seem wasteful, but no more so than a male human ejaculation when 350 million sperm may be released, and men have control over where their sperm is going.

The minute grains of pollen are tough and prepared for a journey of a few inches or many miles. They have a coating that protects and keeps the contents dormant for hours, weeks or even thousands of years, until softened by moisture in female parts of the same plant species. The shapes of pollen grains are elaborate and different for each kind of plant, designed to be recognized and fit into the female parts of their own flower species.

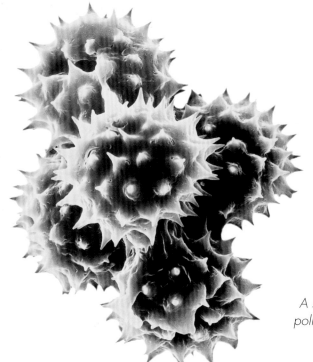

A selection of magnified pollen grains—top, daisy and bottom, iris. Right: Hibiscus

Pollen photos by S. Lowry/University of Ulster.

12

Making it obvious ...

Ariel Skelley

HAWAIIAN SWIMSUITS

... *better than naked*

Lee White/Westlight

NEW YORK · LONDON · PARIS

It is easy to find the female parts on a flower because they are in the center. Just follow the flower stem as it leads directly into the ovary and then farther on to the pollen-receiving parts.

The botanical terms for the female parts are enough to drive a gardener crazy, but the term for an individual unit is carpel. Several carpels fused together make a pistil, the term used in this book.

Stigmas: The Receiving End

At the top of the pistil is the stigma, a receptive area that is often out in the open to catch pollen

Some of the petals have dropped off this lily, so the whole pistil is visible, from the green, oval ovary along the style to the pinkish stigma at the top.

grains. It retains them until it has determined if the pollen is from the right family (how human), and then lets them progress to the ovary. Stigmas are distinctive and each flower species has a different shape. When not needed they tend to be small and unobtrusive, but once the flower is ready to accept pollen there is an exciting change. In many flowers, including honeysuckle and datura, the stigma is situated on the end of a long stem that lunges out to increase the chances of male pollen being trapped. The rounded stigmas of a lily or petunia gleam when ready to catch pollen. The colors of some flowers become intense, the scents grow powerful and the stigmas become dewy and sticky as if yearning for sex. When touched by an insect some violets will secrete a liquid from their stigmas and draw pollen back inside with the moisture. Other stigmas split into several parts, or have hairs, wrinkles or folds to trap pollen. Some types of crocus have beautifully frilled and flaring orange stigmas, hibiscus have five furry pads, zauschneria stigmas are sticky and vincas have woolly knobs.

Once pollen has penetrated the stigmas and start to germinate, pollination has officially taken place. The flower could be said to have succeeded but this is only mating. A lot more has to happen before any offspring are produced.

Styles and Pollen Tubes

Most flowers have a tubular conduit called a style connecting the stigma to the ovary, the pollen's ultimate destination. Either one or many pollen grains grow tubes down the style. The whole pollen grain, however, does not travel down a ready-made tunnel like a train in a subway. Rather the bulk of the grain stays at the top of the stigma while it extends a pollen tube down which the nucleus progresses. On the way it may be helped or inhibited by chemicals. It may die or lose its way. It is not clear how it knows which way to grow toward the female eggs in the ovary, a voyage of several inches in some large flowers, but the male and female cells are able to chemically communicate at this stage. Only the strongest and most vigorous male genes will evade the barriers and survive the journey.

A peony flower grows older. When the flower opens, the vigorous anthers are ready to dispense pollen. But as the flower ages, the anthers and petals fall off, and the green ovaries swell.

Ovaries

The ovary is where the eggs may be fertilized and develop. Immature plant ovaries are inconspicuous small green havens, where the plant's children, their keys to immortality, are protected.

Inside are the eggs, called ovules (either one or many), arranged in various patterns on placental tissue. Rows of green peas in a pod are just one of hundreds of arrangements. Kept moist and well nourished, they remain tiny, waiting for an incoming sperm. It takes one pollen grain to fertilize each pea, "seed" or ovule in the ovary after some complex cell division and fusion. Then the plant is finally pregnant and more dramatic changes take place. The male parts of the flower, no longer needed, wither and drop off. The petals too have lost their jobs, and as the colors fade they crumple and fall.

16

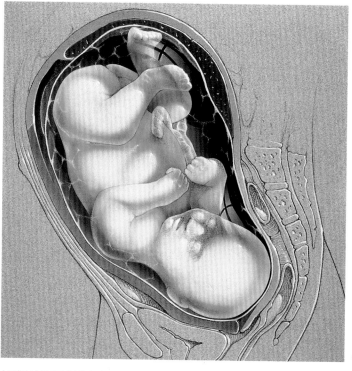

Top: Human fetus in uterus
Bottom: Seeds inside peppers

Illustration by Michael Kress-Russick

Ovules

Meanwhile, the ovary goes into full female production mode. It swells, taking up moisture and nutrients from the plant's roots as the fertilized ovules grow into seeds, and manufactures a potential new plant packaged in a tough shell with its own nutritional supply. The plant puts a good deal of energy into seed production. The ovary grows fatter each day and turns into the seed head so familiar to gardeners. Many people find them unsightly and snip the dead flower heads off, giving the fertilized plant an "abortion." Gardeners who want to promote more blooms on plants also cut off the head as this stimulates an effort by the plant to replace its lost seeds by producing more flowers and starting the process over. Some plants, particularly annuals that have only one summer to complete a whole life cycle, are programmed to bloom for months if the plant is dead-headed. On perennials secondary shoots and buds will often form on healthy plants once mature ovaries have been removed. Bulbs, however, are less adaptable. It may take a year or two to grow cell tissues to form a flower underground, so even when dead blooms are clipped off it is usually not possible for a plant to grow more flowers until the following season. Of course many flowers are never fertilized and the ovules and ovaries do not develop further. Like the pollen grains that never leave the anther they become extra material that the plant no longer needs.

Some flowers, like gentians, have multiple ovaries.

Poppy ovaries ripening in the sunshine

American robin's nest

Other Flower Parts

Evolutionary chance and the need to innovate have led plants to produce flowers with other structures too.

◀ SEPALS—Looking from the outside of a flower inward, the first thing one may see are leafy sepals. Before the flower opens the sepals are wrapped around the bud protecting it. Hairy sepals help deter marauding insects and deflect hot sunrays. Many sepals are green and look like a whorl of small leaves at the base of the flower.

PETALS—Inside the sepals and around the sexual organs ▶ are usually petals. The primary job of petals is to send a distinctive advertising message to a live pollen carrier. A secondary job may be protecting the reproductive parts from weather and offering shelter to a carrier. Different flower families have different numbers, colors, sizes and shapes of petals that make the flower easily recognizable to a pollinator.

◀ TEPALS—Tulips, and plenty of other flowers, don't have green, leaflike sepals; but colored sepals and petals that look very similar.

BRACTS—Plants like bougainvillea, poinsettia and flower- ▶ ing dogwood have bunches of homely little flowers that might never be noticed if it wasn't for the colorful, leafy bracts that surround each bloom. The bracts act like extra petals, sending a signal to an insect or bird. Durable bracts hold up better than waxy petals, and plants with bracts are usually in bloom for a long time, maybe for weeks, making them popular garden and houseplants.

Rob Proctor

Nectaries

At the base of many petals are glands where flowers produce edible, sweet nectar in order to get a sexual carrier to visit. Some of these nectaries are minute and hard for gardeners to see, but they are just right for small insects. Other flowers produce quantities of nectar that collect in deep tubes and feed bigger pollinators. Nasturtiums have just one spur with a narrow entrance guarded by the flower's sexual organs—there is no way a pollinator can get to the nectar without touching them. The five petals of columbines project in five spurs to the back of the flower, with each spur containing a nectary that encourages thirsty hummingbirds. Where there are several nectaries, insects may have to shift positions in order to feed at each one, further increasing the chances of pollen being collected or deposited. Nectaries are often shielded by hairs, lips, doors or projections on the petals that help prevent theft by unwanted visitors and raindrops from diluting the nectar.

Top: Nasturtium
Left: Columbine

2 SEXUAL ORIENTATION

The whole subject of sexual orientation in humans arouses intense anxiety and emotions as civilizations attribute various moral values to sexual behavior. For plants the matter is merely one of adapting for survival. Being male in the morning and female in the afternoon helps certain plants reproduce. Some plants need pollen from another flowering plant in their family, while others can fertilize themselves. There are advantages and disadvantages to each technique.

When plants pollinate themselves all that happens is that male pollen from the stamens lands by accident or design on the female stigma inside the same flower, or on a sibling flower in the same plant. The advantage of plants having sex with themselves, which some botanists call "selfing," is that the new plants are clones. Generations of plants will be the same unless some chance mutation of the genes occurs. A clone can be a good thing if the plant is flourishing, but if certain circumstances, such as climate or human activity, change and the plant does not adapt, then it could become extinct.

If plants cross-pollinate, that is if male pollen from one flower fertilizes the female parts on another flower of the same species but on a separate plant, then the genes from both plants will be mixed and a slightly altered plant will be produced. If the new plant is better it may thrive and reproduce again; if worse it may die young. The majority of plants are cross-pollinated and the various arrangements of their sexual organs and behavior are partly efforts to promote cross-pollination and prevent selfing.

How to Avoid Incest

Most human cultures discourage interbreeding among immediate family members, and the benefits of outbreeding have long been recognized. Natural selection has produced plants that try to prevent selfing while they broadcast their pollen to other plants. Plants do this partly by growing in combinations of sexual orientation such as those in the photographs on this page.

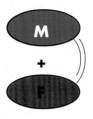

Begonia has separate male flowers and female flowers on the same plant.

Most hollies have male flowers on one tree and female flowers on another tree.

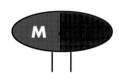

Sprekelia has male and female organs together in each flower.

*Opposite Page
Top: Cineraria*

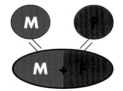

Many squash plants have complex sex lives. They first have male flowers, then female flowers with sterile male anthers and finally sometimes flowers with both viable male and female organs. The flowers appear similar to bees who try and collect pollen from all.

Bisexual Flowers

The *Oxford English Dictionary* says that a hermaphrodite is a person or animal with characteristics of both sexes. It should include flowers. More flowers have both male and female parts than any other combination. It sounds dangerously intimate but, in fact, it is a realistic and flexible arrangement for providing satisfactory intercourse. When flowers are grouped on one stem, or are close together on one plant, they have ways to prevent themselves from being fertilized by the pollen of a sibling. Some have flower buds that open at different times. Other flowers prevent their own pollen penetrating their own stigmas by taking turns at being the dominant sex.

MEN AND BOYS FIRST

Self-fertilization can be avoided if the stamens and pistil in a single flower are sexually active at different times. On some plants the flower starts out in a youthful male mode, with showy anthers shedding pollen while the female pistil is still immature and the stigma unreceptive. Perhaps the stigma will be small and tucked inside the flower so no family pollen lands on the virgin surface, or it will be held out of the way as the style leans over to one side. After a few hours or days, when the male pollen has had an opportunity to be dispersed by a pollinator, the flower switches over to a female mode. Then the pistil grows longer, reaching beyond the male parts so it contacts the incoming pollinators first, and the stigma at the tip becomes receptive. Meanwhile, the male stamens may deactivate, become limp and bend over to the side. Garden flowers that are first male and then female include most mints, penstemons, evening primroses, fireweed and honeysuckles.

Left: A mint

The changing sexual dominance of a Peruvian lily. Here with some tepals removed to show inside. Left: opening in male phase. Center: male phase with some anthers ready to let loose pollen. Right: in female phase with pistil elongated and stigma receptive

WOMEN FIRST

Other types of garden plants do things the other way around: the flowers are female for a while, or until pollinated, then the male organs take over. Plants such as magnolias, water lilies, pasque flowers and the vine Dutchman's pipe have flowers that start out as girls.

MAKING IT IMPOSSIBLE

In some bisexual flowers everything is ready to perform at once, but selfing is avoided by strategically placed chemical barriers. Anemones are an example of flowers that can't fertilize themselves even if their stigmas are covered with their own pollen grains, because the female pistils chemically recognize them and will not let them penetrate as far as the ovaries.

Other flowers are constructed with physical barriers. Many garden flowers have receptive stigmas on long stems, and male anthers on shorter stems below, so the pollen is unlikely to fall or be deposited on that flower's own stigmas. Roses have about a hundred stamens in a ring surrounding one pistil. The outside row of stamens become sexually active first. They grow erect, lean away from the stigma, shed pollen on a carrier, then grow flaccid as the next row takes over. This system discourages self-pollination even though the organs are so close together. There are some plants that are not particular about how they get pregnant as long as it happens eventually. When the petals shrivel on these flowers they may squash the male and female organs together, creating a chance for self-pollination at the last minute. Sun roses (*Helianthemum* sp.) are an example of flowers that are usually cross-pollinated, but in gloomy weather, when few insects are about, they can self-pollinate when the flower closes.

Left: The sexually discriminating anemone
Bottom: Hellebores are females first.

David Miltz

23

Segregated Sexes

There are plants that have separate male, or mostly male flowers, and nearby female, or mostly female flowers. For instance, the familiar spring primroses (Primula) grow as two separate kinds of plants. The mostly female ones have a long style and a stigma peeping out through a hole in the middle of the flower, called a pin-eyed primrose. It has very small stamens but it is essentially a female flower. Thrum-eyed primroses are the opposite, with five male anthers sticking out of the hole. Insects fly from one flower to the next and there is little danger of the aptly named primrose pollinating itself.

Other plants, such as date trees, tackle reproduction like most animals do, that is with separate male plants and female plants. Ancient Mediterranean civilizations understood that in order to produce dates from certain palms it took at least two trees. They are said to have mastered the art of collecting pollen from male date palms and dusting it on the flowers of female palms thousands of years ago. Modern gardeners who want to attract birds with berries need to be just as aware of the sex of some of their trees and shrubs.

Some gardeners consider sex messy and tiresome so they have single sex trees that can't reproduce. Female cottonwoods send their seeds flying through the air with copious white fluffy "cotton," and female Kentucky coffee trees drop large brown pods. These and many other trees are often sold in sterile or male form so their passions can be contained by tidy gardeners.

SELECTING YOUR OWN SEX

What determines the sex of new plants that could grow into either males or females? It appears that the environment is sometimes the answer. Seedlings stressed in a harsh, dry environment become males, while those receiving more favorable conditions become female. In terms of energy invested, it is cheaper for a plant to produce pollen than bear the burden of offspring, so being male in hard times and female in good times makes sense. Jack-in-the pulpits are familiar garden perennials that change sex. The first year they are planted and getting established they are usually male. The second year they grow bigger and may become female. To turn your "Jack" into a "Jill" just pamper it.

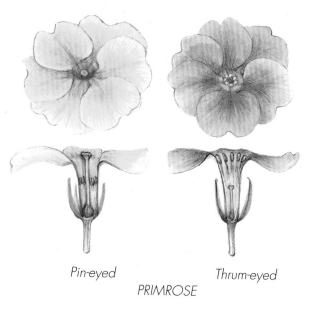

Pin-eyed   Thrum-eyed

PRIMROSE

"Selfing"

Plants designed to self-pollinate save energy by not having to attract and reward pollen carriers with expensive food and perks. They can afford to be inconspicuous with little flowers and thus are not particularly popular in the garden. Other plants have flowers that have evolved to be cross-pollinated but who hedge their bets when conditions are poor and there are no carrier visits. They might self-pollinate when first open, or even while still in the bud, then wait for a cross-pollinator. Some wait in vain. Others pollinate themselves as a last resort just before they shrivel up. Either the male or female parts change direction and swoop toward the other, snuggling up so a transfer of pollen onto the stigma can take place.

Violets can produce two sorts of flowers. Some are hidden under the leaves. They are small, semideveloped flowers that never open but "self" during early spring and fall when few insects are around. The rest are showy, cross-pollinated flowers that bloom when the weather is warmer. Buttercups are usually cross-pollinated, but when it rains and insects are not flying about, they stay open, fill with water and their pollen floats onto their own stigmas.

Some plants allow male pollen from both other plants and their own stamens to penetrate the stigmas, but favor cross-pollination by producing chemicals that make sure that the pollen tubes from the other plant grow toward the ovary faster than their own, so the other pollen wins the race and cross-pollination has an edge if there is a chance of both happening.

There are plants that have spent millions of years adapting to just one pollinator. They could be called devoted and faithful. Monkshood (*Aconitum* sp.), a handsome plant with distinguished flowers, is only fertilized by bumblebees, and if none are around it will eventually "self" rather than die "unfulfilled." Daisies and hundreds of other species have been promiscuous for years and any living pollinator will do. They don't need to have especially distinctive or memorable flowers, because they are visited by many kinds of insects and never have the problem of being starved for sex.

Top: Bellflower anthers ejaculate pollen onto the female organs before the flower even opens. This might seem premature, but instead of the flower being self-pollinated, the pistil elongates and exposes the pollen to a visiting insect, then finally the stigma divides and becomes receptive to pollen from another flower.
Center: Promiscuous dandelions are fertlized by a multitude of insects.
Bottom: Monkshood flowers are faithful to bumblebees

Don Sweitzer

3 THE ULTIMATE ADVERTIS

Like all living things, plants have to struggle to survive on our planet. They have to compete with others for the most soil space, water, light and air, and unless they are wind pollinated, they have to fight with neighboring plants for the attention of sexual partners. As plants reach puberty they advertise their health, size and species while growing into a recognizable shape. When they are finally ready to reproduce the blossoms surrounding the sexual parts send a message to passing pollinators that the plant is ready to exchange something worthwhile if the pollinator will only visit.

Mass displays are perennially popular, but individual people and plants have a hard time getting noticed when regimented in groups like these.

Wang's
Kitchen
chinese cuisine
DINING ROOM AND CARRY OUT

KFC

KFC®

NOW
HIRING

The David E. Bailey
Construction Co.
980-0440

COSMOPOLITAN

April 1994 • $2.95

YOU'RE
FIRED.
A Realistic
Survival
Plan

The
Enduring,
Enigmatic
Charm of
Jacqueline
Kennedy
Onassis

Mel
Gibson
Raunchy,
Rip-roaring
Superstar

COSMO'S
Guide
to Never
Looking
as Old as
You Are

27

Claude Steelman

How to Attract Attention

Paul Grebliunas

Left: Brazilian carnival dancer in costume performs
at the Rio de Janeiro Carnival.
Top right: Male sage grouse puffing out his air sacs
and tail in a spring courting ritual
Top left (opposite page): Malva with striking display
Right: Baboons send an obvious message
when they are ready for a partner.

Rob Proctor

as a field of flowers

a fragrance as fresh

India Stock

from THE HEART OF NATURE

in a Competitive Field

SuperStock

29

Advertising with Color

Nearly all pollinators fly so their first impression of plants is from a distance. As they look down on various shades of green, other colors attract their attention and let pollinators know that a plant is in flower. Color is the most obvious signal from far away, but color is a matter of who is perceiving it. Most people see the whole spectrum of colors in this book; birds and many insects may observe only some of them, while bees can see short-wavelength ultraviolet that we can only see with the help of special lighting. Smell also attracts pollinators; for example, bees cannot see red colors but may be drawn to scarlet roses by their scent.

Potentilla as perceived by:
humans …   *bees …*   *hummingbirds …*   *beetles.*

30

Flower colors that pollinators prefer

When selecting plants for your garden you may want to consider what color pollinators prefer.

BEES: yellow, blue, purple, ultraviolet
BUTTERFLIES: red, orange, yellow, pink
FLIES: green, lime, white, cream
CARRION-EATING FLIES: maroon, brown
HUMMINGBIRDS: red, orange, purple-red

The following are just samples of the many interesting ways insects interact with garden colors. Bees love yellows; they appear as warm colors to them. The red wavelengths are too long for bees to see, so what we think of as purples, bees see without the red, that is as shades of blue. Some primroses, and other flowers we see as yellow but bees perceive as a mixture of yellow and ultraviolet that is called "bee purple." Flowers that look plain white to us may appear white, as some daisies do, because they have air pockets between their cells or because they are reflecting back to us the primary colors of the light spectrum—red, green and blue. Some flowers that we call white appear as ultraviolet to bees, and plenty of flowers have stripes, spots and shading of ultraviolet on their petals as guides to bees, that we, unfortunately, cannot admire in our flower beds.

LIGHT SPECTRUM:

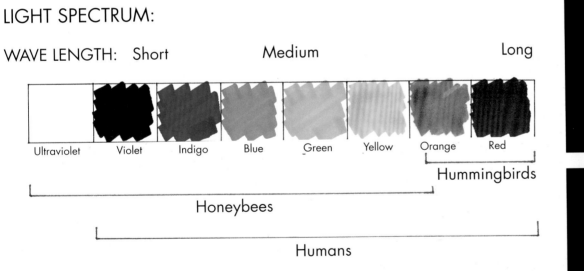

WAVE LENGTH: Short   Medium   Long

Ultraviolet   Violet   Indigo   Blue   Green   Yellow   Orange   Red

Hummingbirds

Honeybees

Humans

Top: Flower photographed under sun light.
Bottom: Same flower photographed under ultraviolet light.

31

Sybil Bashor

How plants make different flower colors

Plants are genetically programmed to produce colors with chemicals in the cells of their blossoms. The chemicals vary according to the soil and are also influenced by temperature and climate. As a child I enjoyed burying English "coppers" (pennies) around our pink hydrangeas in an effort to make them produce blue flowers. There are now substances on the market to create the same effect. Many flowers, especially those with thick, waxy blooms, have petals with several layers of cells in different colors, producing a shimmering effect. The velvety blossoms of flowers, such as gloxinias and pansies, appear to have such rich and sparkling color because the surface of the petals are not flat but corrugated to catch and reflect light. Flowers with intense black areas, such as some poppies, have layers of all the different colored cells in them.

Top: Gloxinia
Middle: Pansies
Bottom: Oriental poppy

Bee Guides . . . . . .

The competition to woo flighty pollinators is so intense that plants use visual, tactile and fragrant aids to gain maximum advertising impact. Bee guides, also called nectar or honey guides, are the colored stripes, spots and markings on petals. They help pollinators find the flowers quickly and vividly mark the spot where a fast meal is available. Many flowers are two-toned, often with a golden-glow surrounding the nectaries. There are flowers with invisible lines or dots of scent impregnated on the petals that grow stronger toward the nectar. In case some pollinators still have not got the message, there are flowers with actual grooves on the petals that guide long tongues past the sexual organs down to the reward. Lilies, like some people, hardly know when to stop when it comes to clamoring for attention. They importune with garish displays of scent, bee guides and lavish decorations, but they are often the flowers we love the best.

Top Left: Cape primrose with dark stripes pointing to the action
Top middle: Morning glory with a golden throat
Right: Foxglove with attention-seeking spots

Targeted Designs

The bull's eye or target design is a familiar message shouting "look here!" The concentric rings of verbena flowers send the same message. Lilies and day lilies often have ridged tepals as well as spots to guide pollinators, such as the Vinca.

TARGET

STOP
What You Are Doing

Road signs and
flowers send a
similar message.

Viper's bugloss and wallflowers exhibiting color changes

Changing color after sex

Fortunately it is not possible to tell by looking at a person's face if they recently had sex. Not so with some flowers, who send a message when they have been pollinated that the affair is over and nothing more will be offered. This saves the pollinator from wasting its time and energy hunting in the flower for food, and gives the rest of the plant's flowers an opportunity for reproduction, while the fertilized flowers get on with the business of producing seeds.

Some plants encourage innumerable insect visits. Others have ways of signaling that they are finished with sex. For instance, the flowers of Spanish bayonet (yucca) and wine-cup (*Callirhoe involucrata*) close, and those of orchids shrivel up quickly. Other plants have individual flowers that may be sexually satisfied, but withering afterward could spoil the rest of the plant's long-distance advertising display, so the flowers hold their basic shape and color a little longer while subtle changes take place that can only be seen on close inspection. For example, the scent disappears, nectar is no longer available or the look of the flower alters somewhat as pollinators pry open petals or set offspring loaded mechanisms. Blue bonnets (*Lupinus texensis*) have a white or yellow spot that lures bees to their favorite color. After the flower is pollinated the spot turns red, a color the bees cannot see.

Panayoti Kelaidis

Top: The sizzling yellow blooms of the red-hot-poker are in heat, while the younger red blooms above are just glowing embers.
Middle: The pink buds of chiming bells turn into blue flowers when the plant is ready.
Bottom: This species of shrub verbena has yellow young flowers, orange middle-aged flowers and red elderly flowers.

Advertising with Scents

A bower of sweet-smelling roses.

After color, the next most important advertisement a flower can put on is a good smell. The two scents that lure animals most effectively suggest food or sex, and pollinators favor variations on these two themes. Sweet food smells are beloved by hungry bees, butterflies, moths, wasps and some flies. The odor of the opposite sex attracts lusting insects, and the rotting-flesh-and-feces type of smells are relished by insects like carrion-eating flies or certain beetles searching for a place to lay their eggs. (There is more about these distasteful creatures in Chapter 5.)

Most insects have an exquisite sense of smell, far more sensitive than ours, so flowers that smell only vaguely to the average gardener may waft a strong message to a bee or a fly. Anyone eating outdoors knows how quickly wasps can detect food odors, descend out of nowhere and attempt to eat one's meal. When blindfolded, gardeners may be able to distinguish the sweet smells of flowers like hyacinth, paper-white narcissus, rose, lily-of-the-valley, lavender or violet, perhaps half a dozen all together. Only a few people can identify more, but collecting honeybees have to sort out and remember hundreds of flower fragrances, sometimes from a good distance.

It costs energy for flowers to produce scents, and they would not do it unless is was an effective way of communicating. Promiscuous flowers, those that encourage many different kinds of insects, tend to give off generic, sweet, light odors that are appealing to a wide range of pollinators. More selective flowers scent the air with their own distinctive smell, either all the time or just at the time of the day when they are ready. The most powerful sweet perfumes are emitted by the flowers that attract night-flying moths and bats. On moonless nights a flower's scent may be the only way of letting a pollinator know where the flower's food is located.

On languid summer evenings one of my favorite entertainments is watching the petals of the pale yellow evening primroses spring open and the sphinx moths flying in to collect the nectar, sometimes impatiently nuzzling the buds, forcing them to unfold faster. Other flowers, like white tobacco plants, are well worth growing in front of a window so the glorious scents creep into the house on summer nights.

The image of sun-warmed roses with fat, floppy-petalled blossoms exuding heady smells as they contentedly let buzzing bees collect and distribute their plentiful pollen is a sexy and satisfying scene. Fragrant lavender walks, heliotrope bouquets, gardenias pinned to the front of a dress; the perfume industry would be the first to tell us that it is not only bees that are attracted to flower smells. Humans find them alluring too, and not because they smell of supper. Certain orchids are not above emitting smells with the same allure as a female insect. This arouses the appropriate male insects from all around, encouraging them to visit the flower for sex, while it is only the flower that sometimes succeeds in that regard. Some flowers have addictive scents that keep insects returning to them over and over again, while others have drugging perfumes that seem to make insects entranced and loathe to leave. That smell would certainly sell well in the human market if it could be bottled. One of the oddest smells given off by flowers is the yeasty stench of a particular South African protea. They are pollinated by mice, so their grainy smell works well for them. Not all flowers go to the expense of producing perfumes. Flowers pollinated by hummingbirds for instance don't need to be fragrant because these birds have practically no sense of smell at all.

Four aromas that can awaken human passions: viburnum, rose, lilac and heliotrope

Advertising with Shapes

Once a pollinator has seen the colors of flowers from a distance, and possibly smelled them too, it may fly in for a closer look. Then the details of the floral display become obvious. The way the flowers grow on the stem, the number of flowers, the size and shape of the group and each individual flower send an important message and determine who enters it. Pollinators soon discover that certain flowers offer food and suit their shape and characteristics admirably, while other flowers are no help at all. The food may be impossible to reach, the shape may offer no place to land or the location may be unfavorable. Every flower on earth is adapted to the wind, water or some animal pollinator, and it has a very limited time in which to sell its advantages to a series of picky passers-by.

Common flower shapes that attract pollinators:

open, sun warmed bowls;

selective entrances for long beaks and long tongues;

shelter from rain and predators;

landing platforms for bees;

landing platforms for bees, flies, beetles and butterflies

Moss roses

California poppies

Bowl-Shaped Flowers

The simplest and oldest design for flowers is a group of petals forming an up-turned bowl shape. They attract many insects. These flowers are easily seen from the air; the bowl provides shelter as it focuses the sun's rays, creating a slightly higher temperature than the surroundings, and the stem may even turn so the flower tracks the sun. The extra warmth inside the flower bowl can speed up seed production, especially important in colder climates like Alaska and at high altitudes where plants have to reproduce in a very short season. Bowl-shaped flowers are popular with many short-tongued insects who like to feed in the open, but in poor weather the flowers' pollen is liable to be damaged unless it can close quickly. Flowers such as rose and peonies sometimes have semiclosed bowls that provide a sheltered, cozy haven for insects while the in-curving petals partially protect the pollen from rain.

Trumpet and Bell-Shaped Flowers

Both the width of the trumpet bloom and the angle it hangs at are adaptations that attract certain pollinators. Many groups of flowers have petals that are fused together into a tube, trumpet or funnel shape. For instance, upward facing phlox flowers have a narrow tube of fused petals that flare out at the top. This shape attracts long-tongued insects, particularly butterflies, who like to feed on the flat area, while the phlox flower tubes are narrow enough to protect the pollen and nectar from rain and unwanted insects. The outward-facing, trumpet-shape of flowers, such as daffodils, protects the sexual parts from most moisture and wind while it encourages low-flying bees. Flowers with fused petals that hang down like a bell shed rain like an umbrella and many insects are unable or unwilling to fly up inside them. Medium-sized, bell-shaped drooping flowers, such as foxgloves, are a favorite of honey- and bumblebees, who have the ability to climb inside and collect pollen while hanging like mountaineers. Bees and other insects like to shelter from wind and rain, and some even spend the night inside hanging flowers. Very thin tubular blossoms, such as those of red fairy trumpet (*Ipomopsis aggregata*), exclude fat bees, but are exactly the right length and width for the beaks of hummingbirds.

Foxglove

Lily

Daffodil

Lemon peel clematis

Beauty bush

Penstemon

Landing Platforms

Bees pollinate more flowers than other insects because so many native flowers are adapted to their needs. Bees like to stop at a flower to feed and collect food so landing platforms where they can put their feet down first are very popular. Bee flowers often have a large lower petal at the front of the flower that offers a free parking space. It has to be sturdy to stand up to a number of bustling, heavy bees and orientated so that when the bee arrives it is already headed in the right direction. A desirable bee plant, such as a delphinium can look like a busy airport with bees flying in, landing and taking off. Butterflies also stop flying to feed but they prefer a flat surface with a view in all directions.

Top: Pink
Aeroplane: Pilot/owner: Michael Baldwin; photographer: Walt Barbo
Bottom: Greek foxglove
Right: Yarrow
Far right: Coneflowers

An Age-Old Question: Whether to Conceal …

Whether sexual parts are more appealing hidden or revealed is a question that has been mulled over by men and women since time immemorial. Flowers that are attracting partners with food, not sex, have evolved in both ways. Some flowers are structured so that insects access the food as easily as lunch spread on a picnic table, while others hide all they have to offer.

Japack/Westlight

46

or Reveal?

Model: Bryan Wright

Lily by Rob Proctor

47

Barely Concealed

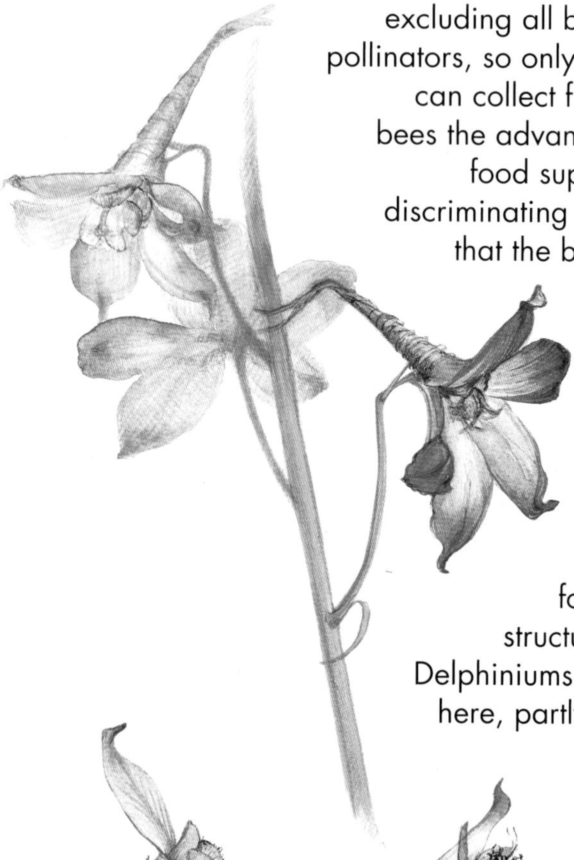

Some plants promote cross-pollination by excluding all but certain species of pollinators, so only a bee, for instance, can collect from them. This gives bees the advantage of an exclusive food supply, and the plant a discriminating pollinator. It ensures that the bee prefers that plant and visits similar ones often, transferring its pollen reliably, rather than wasting it on incompatible species. Excluding features take many forms, including size, structure, smell and color. Delphiniums, like the one drawn here, partly conceal what they have to offer, excluding unsophisticated insects. The flowers have small petal-like appendages covering the sexual parts and orifice leading to the nectar. The effect is of a woolly cod piece, much like those worn in fifteenth-century Europe, here displayed by Charles V in a famous portrait by Titian in the Prado Museum, Madrid, Spain.

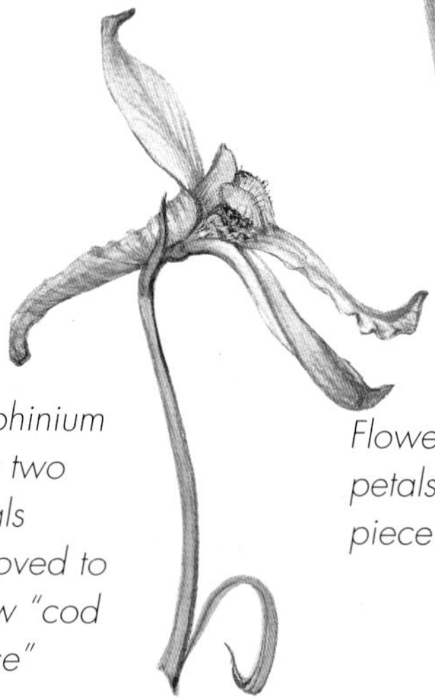

Charles V by Titian

Delphinium with two petals removed to show "cod piece"

Flower with most petals and cod piece removed

Both people and plants exploit the advantages of semiconcealed sexual parts.

Totally Concealed

Some flowers have their sexual parts and nectar completely hidden in a chamber, which can only be reached by strong and intelligent pollinators who learn how to operate the contraptions by trial and error. The weight of the bee landing on the lower lip of this red snapdragon causes the hinged petals to drop open, so the bee can climb inside and reach the nectar and pollen, while it accidentally carries pollen to pistils from one flower to the next. Once inside the flower the bee cannot see out, and its rear is vulnerable to predators, but most female collecting bees are protected with stingers in their tails.

Elaborately Shaped Flowers with Concealed Parts

There are hundreds of members of the pea family, all with slightly different shaped flowers, but most share a similar method of interacting with bees so a delivery of their pollen takes place. Garden flowers like false indigo (*Baptisia*), lupine (*Lupinus*) and sweet pea (*Lathyrus odoratus*) have a large upper petal, appropriately called a banner, as it does the advertising. The pair of side petals are called wings, but stirrups might be a better word. They help advertise and provide a pair of mounts for the bee's feet to ride the flower and hold on while searching for food. The two long narrow petals clapped together hiding the sexual parts are called a keel, as in boat. Bees lured to these flowers by color and the aroma of food straddle the keel with their heads facing toward the flower.

Left: Lupine
Bottom: False indigo

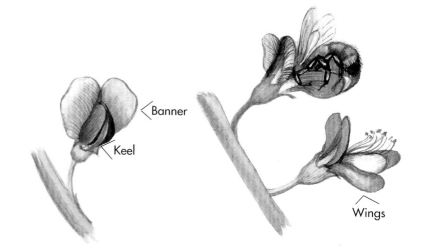

Speedy Delivery

Some pea flowers have stamens that are partly fused into a hollow rod surrounding the pistil, and this whole mechanism is situated in the keel under tension. The weight of a bee sets off a pistonlike action that squeezes a portion of pollen on the insect's underside. In some pea species the rod is positioned in a hole in the point of the keel; in others the two halves of the keel split open and the stiff male and female parts rear up to receive the pollen from a previous flower and deliver their own pollen on the the unsuspecting bee, sometimes with a thump on the furry, soft belly. The flower parts commonly return to their original position after each bee visit, but in plants like alfalfa, the tiny purple flowers only have one chance as the spring cannot be reset.

The mint and figwort family of flowers, among others, also have carefully aimed sexually delivery and receptive systems. Most of them have evolved to deposit pollen from anthers onto bees' hairy backs, but according to the flower structure pollen can stick on the insects' tongues, eyes, heads, feet or everywhere. The idea is that the food is so important the pollinator either will not notice, have time or care enough to remove every grain of pollen before visiting the next flower of the same species. The male anthers of mountain laurel flowers (*Kalmia latifolia*) favor alacrity over accuracy. They are tucked into the petals until the weight of a bee suddenly dislodges them, flinging powdery pollen in all directions.

The sexual parts of the garden broom flowers are coiled around and unleashed under the weight of a guest.

THE MOST HIGHLY SPECIALIZED FLOWERS

Some of the most recent flowers to evolve on this planet are the most highly specialized. They allow only particular insects to obtain food from them, and to get the food the insect has to be in a precise position. An example is the beautiful blue or white monkshood that can only be pollinated by bumblebees, or by human intervention. In the wild, monkshood will not thrive unless bumblebees live in the area. Many wild orchids and other complex flowers also need to be pollinated by a particular species of bee, wasp or other insect.

Hairy Flowers

Hair and hairiness play a part in human attractiveness. Most flowers have hairs on them too, although some are only visible under a microscope. They commonly play a defensive role, but there are other compensations. Hairs on flowers can be as distinctive and memorable to a pollinator as the shape. On some plants they guard access to the nectar, pointing toward the flower entrance like so

many tiny spears, preventing unwanted small insects from sneaking in. Many flowers have hairy female receptive parts that trap the male pollen. In some pea family blossoms hairs even sweep up loose pollen from the floor of the keel, exhibiting an economy and tidiness many people can relate to. Flower sepals and the outside of the ovary often have bristly hairs that help protect the flower and unformed seeds inside. Hairs on both the foliage and flowers protect against rain, heat, cold, dehydration and, if sufficiently unpalatable, against the flower being eaten by a predator, such as a caterpillar.

Bunches of hairs on flowers come in a range of textures and colors that appear to us as decorative, but that is not their only purpose. Bearded irises, delphiniums and a number of other garden flowers have woolly pads of hairs displayed on the lower petals that have to tickle the undersides of feeding insects as they reach toward the nectar. Tufts of bright yellow hairs can look like a good pollen source. Mounds of brown or black hairs resemble another insect already foraging at the flower.

Top left: Woolly pasque flower petals help protect the bloom in poor spring weather.
Top middle: Penstemons usually have four stamens bearing pollen hidden in the recess at the top of the flower, and one hairy, sterile stamen exposed in the mouth of the blossom.
Right: Delphinium exhibiting tufts of hairs

Making the Size Fit the Client

small mammals pollinate these exotic treasures. At high altitude on windy mountainsides, where only strong bumblebees or sturdy small insects can sally forth, short plants produce small flowers. Temperate climates tend to produce flowers sized somewhere between the two extremes.

Bunching hundreds of tiny flowers on a single stem, however, has many advantages for a plant and the pollinator. Like a guest grazing at a party buffet, the pollinator saves time and energy by staying in one place surrounded by a good supply of food. It only has to take a step to reach the next mouthful. Besides, diminutive flowers can be grouped together to make a display that attracts pollinators from far away, and continues to bloom for a long period as the flowers open in sequence. Having tiny flowers with minute sexual parts is no disgrace in the plant world.

The size of a plant's flower depends on the size of pollinators available in a plant's native area. Hungry mammals and birds are lured to large flowers by big rewards of nectar. Insects are content with smaller flowers and smaller bribes. In hot, humid, sheltered tropical climates with a wealth of insects, including giant butterflies and moths, plants can afford to invest in huge flowers. In northern climates, where we have to admire these plants in greenhouses or try to grow them as house plants, we can only imagine what great insects, colorful birds or

WITH THE HELP OF A FEW FRIENDS

In many cultures groups of unattached young men and women gather together in public, on the street or a dance floor to make an obvious show of seeking partners.

On their own they might be insignificant, but in a gang they command attention. In a similar way many plants produce groups of small flowers close together, called an inflorescence, and with the help of a few "siblings" flaunt their offerings for pollinators who might not notice them otherwise.

There are many different botanical names for the way flowers are grouped together on a stem. They include flowers that grow in pairs, in bunches or in columns like prince's plume, in flat-topped groupings like Queen Anne's lace, or tight mounds or balls of flowers like alliums.

Flat-topped inflorescences and long, fat groupings such as those of butterfly bush (*Buddleia*) or lilacs (*Syringa*) are favorites of butterflies because they can look around while they feed. Such shapes also provide a perch for small birds and a meeting place for masses of small insects whose tongues just fit into the small flowers. The carrot family (*Umbelliferae*), which includes the familiar garden herbs coriander, cumin and dill all have thousands of minute whitish petaled flowers popular with flies and other tiny insects. Each flower has male and female parts. Inside the ovary is a single ovule that, when fertilized and grown, becomes the herb seed that cooks love.

On mound-shaped inflorescences, the outside flowers mature first and are often larger, which makes the display bigger and more effective, or they may just have larger petals on the periphery of the group. But these outside flowers are sometimes sterile, as the English say, "all show and no go." The fertile sibling flowers in the center open in series, making the inflorescence attractive over a long period of time.

Top: Cleome
Center: Dame's rocket
Bottom: Allium

55

Sex in Columns

Garden flowers growing in columns like hyacinths, gladioli, larkspurs, salvias and sages have flowers that open at the bottom of the group first, while the top ones are still in bud. Flying insects and birds start on lower flowers where the food is most plentiful, then systematically search the plant for nectar toward the top. If the flowers are arranged spirally around the spike, bees can be seen circling higher and higher as they explore each flower in turn. Blazing stars (*Liatris* sp.) are unusual, as their flowers open at the top of the column first. Either way, if all the flowers were open at once the whole grouping might last only a day or two, and the pollinator could be sated after visiting just one plant; but if only a few flowers are open on any one day the pollinator has to fly from plant to plant, cross-pollinating effectively, and leaving more flowers for another opportunity the next day.

Mullein

Foxtail lily

Blazing star

Composites

Composites are a large group of plants with complex flower structures and promiscuous sex lives. The tiny flowers grow in groups so close together that they look like a single unit, usually with sterile flowers doing the advertising and plainer ones taking care of the reproduction. All daisies (*Bellis*), asters (*Aster*), sunflowers (*Helianthus*), cornflowers (*Centaurea cyanus*), coneflowers (*Rudbeckia*), cosmos (*Cosmos*), inula (*Inula*), yarrows (*Achillea*), zinnias (*Zinnia*), dahlias (*Dahlia*) and chrysanthemums (*Chrysanthemum*) are in this group, along with many others—over 20,000 species altogether.

Why are these plants so common and successful? The composites can be pollinated by hundreds of different short- and long-tongued insects, and it takes only one of them to get the job done. There are infinitely more chances of auspicious fertilization taking place than in more selective breeds. Composite flowers usually last for a long time. They provide plenty of nectar as a reward, and most will pollinate themselves if nothing else does. They are often tough, adaptable plants, easier to grow in the garden than most and include a number of weedy species, such as thistles and knapweed, whose fecundity gardeners may find dreadful.

When the hundreds of tightly grouped flowers are squashed into a great wheel shape they look better, smell stronger, prevent each other from getting dehydrated and provide a better deal for the pollinators. Most composites consist of two types of flowers; big ray flowers on the outside margin and small disc flowers in the middle.

Disc Flowers

Many disc flowers are so small that a magnifier helps to see them. Each miniature bisexual floret is usually a complete flower, with petals joined into a short tube and a stigma, style and an ovary with a single ovule. The male anthers are often joined into a movable collar around the female part, supported on five flexible stems, or filaments. Eons ago the composites were related to campanula flowers (such as hare bells), and some of the tiny disc flowers still act like campanulas, releasing pollen from their anthers before the flower opens, straight onto the immature and unreceptive pistil. The female pistil usually acts like a piston, elongating and pushing the pollen up through the sheath of male anthers and out the top of the flower for delivery to pollinators. In many composite flowers this sex machine is finely tuned, responding to the stimulation of insects by contracting the filaments of the anther collar so that just a measured amount of pollen is ejaculated, sensibly leaving more for subsequent insect visits. It is not until almost all the pollen is pushed out that the female parts mature, and the flower becomes in essence female. Then the stigmas at the top of the style become receptive, usually branching out into two parts (again like campanulas), ready to accept pollen from another flower. If no pollinator appears, the twin branches may circle round so the receptive sticky parts of the stigmas can touch the flower's last remaining grains of its own pollen and fertilize itself. Some garden composites have only disc flowers such as blazing star *(Liatris)*, pussytoes *(Antennaria)*, pearly everlasting *(Anaphalis)* and sage *(Artemisia)*.

Top: Aster
Bottom: Cosmos

Ray Flowers

Many composites have what appear to be showy petals on the outside of the wheel of the flower. In reality each is nearly always sterile or female-only flowers, and their main function is to advertise the homely but fertile flowers on the inside of the wheel. Instead of having separate petals, each flower's petals are often fused into a single, long, attractive blade with ridges down the center, like the ones born by cosmos. Another example is the white daisy, the kind where you pull off the "petals" one by one, asking the age-old question "he loves me?" or "he loves me not?" The plucked petals are actually sterile show pieces (hopefully no reflection on the man in question). Some ray flowers are not flattened but tubular.

Some composites have ray flowers and no disc flowers, such as the lovely blue cupid's dart (*Catananche caerulea*). Each tiny individual flower is fringed and flattened and the sepals are modified into fine hairs called pappus that elongate and fluff out when the single seed is ready to be dispersed, acting like a parachute so the wind can lift it up and blow it away. The outer flowers are usually larger than the inside ones and sometimes sterile. The whole thing folds up tight when it rains.

Top: Daisy
Bottom: A bed full of composite flowers

59

Sex Through the Seasons

In order to outshine neighboring plants, flowers open at different times of the day and year. We call it niche marketing. The well-planned blooming garden is, to a pollinator, a convenience store, offering a variety of food 24 hours a day throughout the season.

Barbie, a quintessential American sex symbol, sits among the crocus. The ovary of these flowers is below ground, where it is protected from frost. Picking a crocus cuts the flower off at the midsection.

SPRING: GETTING A JUMP ON THE COMPETITION

Girls who mature early quickly find out that they attract boys as their female competition is not yet ready. Similarly, elderly people who remain sexually active may have many offers, as some of their contemporaries have died or are no longer interested.

The first spring flowers that bloom each year and the last flowers that manage to survive the onslaughts of winter exploit the same situations. Spring flowers scarcely need to advertise; just being there is enough to get them bombarded by hungry bees out reconnoitering the territory for the hive. The first spring flowers are often small and insignificant, on short stems that have not had time to grow. No matter; gardeners rave over the first appearance of these spring Lolitas. They hardly ever lack a sexual carrier, and indeed some appear quite disheveled after several ravenous bees have crowded into the blossom at once.

Early spring blooms—windflower, forsythia and checkered lily

SUMMER

Flowers that bloom at the height of the summer have to be taller, larger, brighter and smell more appealing than spring blooms. One way summer plants compete is by opening at different times and offering nectar on a regular schedule. Blue chicory (*Chicorium intybus*), for example, opens between about 7 A.M. and noon, offering a morning treat. Ice plant (*Delosperma* sp.) opens as the sun warms its petals at midday. Four-o-clock (*Mirabilis jalapa*), true to its name, is an afternoon feast, while thorn apple (*Datura*) waits until the bees have flown home to their hives and the sun sets before they unfold, luring moths, bats and other nocturnal Lotharios. Some flowers stay open 24 hours a day, but they don't necessarily have nectar available the entire time, so one can often see flowers in the garden appearing to be in the peak of maturity and perfection, but with no pollinators in attendance.

An English summer garden

Late fall flowering plants have the same benefits as early spring flowers. Colchicum (commonly known as naked-boys—*Colchicum autumnale*) bloom when deciduous trees are losing their leaves, many plants are brown and wrinkled and most flowers are just memories. The last bright spots in my garden, obedient plant (*Physotegia*) and orange California poppies (*Eschscholzia californica*), get plenty of attention from me and sleepy bees. They set seed just before the first snows.

Sex for a Day ... or Waiting for a Week

Flower petal textures vary from crisp lilies to crumpled poppies to iridescent jewelweeds (*Impatiens*). Most petal surfaces need to be tough enough to shed rain and withstand a certain amount of abuse from pollinators and wind; but flowers that are available for just a few hours like daylilies don't have to hold up for long and often have fragile or easily bruised blooms. In contrast, some orchids can expect their pollinators to pass by only occasionally and have evolved with thick, waxy petals that retain moisture and stay fresh-looking for up to a month.

Top: Obedient plant
Bottom: Colchicum

Many women might wish their skin looked as perfect as the petals on this amaryllis.

Frank Herholdt

Copying a Successful Competitor

All advertising campaigns are costly and a number of people want the results without the expense. Some companies manufacture copycat products hoping their items will sell along with the well recognized ones they are mimicking. Some plants use this tactic too, pretending to look and smell like another flower. Common wildflowers that have spent thousands of years evolving to produce just the right color, shape, size, smell and food reward for a certain pollinator may have rarer plants growing close by that have such similar attributes that pollinators are fooled into visiting them, but may receive no reward at all. It is a cheap trick, but one that works well enough to have been practiced for millions of years. Other groups of flowers are not patent-breakers but are so similar that all the flowers gain an advantage by looking alike. The familiar yellow bowl shapes of buttercups (*Ranunculus*), cinquefoil (*Potentilla*) and sun roses (*Helianthemum*), among others, are either thriving on the same advertising campaign or have all hit on the same very successful design.

63

4 GREAT BRIBES

Once a plant's advertising has grabbed a pollinator's attention it needs to coax the pollinator into a more intimate relationship, for the whole point of the cross-pollinated flower is lost if the animal does not touch the plant's sexual organs. Plants that depend on live pollinators for their long-term survival have to foster codependency with those pollinators, a dependency so compelling that the pollinators will have to visit them and form a partnership so close that neither can live without the other.

Pollinators inadvertently fulfill their end of the bargain with the only thing flowers want—a sexual transfer of their pollen. What must the plant offer in exchange? Insects and other animals visit plants for a number of reasons, but never because the flowers are pretty. They are seduced with the same offers that work for so many living things: food for themselves and their young, shelter and home-building material, sexual aids and lures and a place to meet the opposite sex. The exchange can be called a bribe, reward, payback or whatever, but the results are the same. The ways plants use bribes are not too different from the ways companies in modern democracies market such things as fast food, liquor and cigarettes.

When a business offers fast food and easy parking customers flock to it. Pollinators fly to flowers for the same reason.

CRITERIA FOR THE MANUFACTURE,
SALES AND DISTRIBUTION OF PLANT BRIBES:

1. **Ease of manufacture:** The bribe should be made using low-cost energy and cheap, readily available ingredients.

2. **Target the market:** The bribe should be targeted at specific, reliable pollinators capable of performing the sexual trade; others should be excluded to avoid unnecessary depletion of resources.

3. **Control of distribution:** Plant should have control over manufacture, timing of sales and amounts distributed. The bribe should be tasty enough so the pollinator wants more, but administered in limited quantities so the pollinator shortly has to seek additional supplies in similar outlets. The right pollinators should be encouraged with an easily recognized display and rewarded with a dependable product distributed at predictable times each day.

4. **Addiction:** Repeat customers are encouraged. If the bribe is delicious, appealing, perhaps addictive and/or necessary for pollinators' survival it will be even more successful.

5. **Bonuses:** If the bribe lures a group of hangers-on, small insects that may not pollinate but at least attract larger pollinators by being bait themselves, that is a plus.

Nectar

Nectar is a food bribe produced by plants that fulfills all of the requirements on the previous page. It is not exactly the same product in all plants but it works brilliantly at attracting pollinators all over the world. Nectar is a liquid containing mostly sugars, with small quantities of amino acids, vitamins and minerals. Its composition varies with the plant, the time of day, weather, age of flower and the pollinator. Hummingbirds need dilute nectar, while other pollinators prefer strong, sticky concentrations. Nectar has many advantages: it is quick to drink, easily absorbed into the system and provides almost instant energy. Many insects and a few birds and mammals have evolved to rely on nectar from flowers as a primary source of carbohydrates.

Early plants exuded excess sugars from their leaves, and some, like laurel, still do. Over time plants specialized so that now many flowers manufacture nectar in various glands or discs that are never far from the sexual organs. These nectaries are not usually visible to the naked eye, but the pools of liquid that collect can sometimes be observed in large flowers. Generations of gardeners have sucked on clover and other flowers, and the nectar in nasturtium spurs can be delicious.

Many pollinators, like animals the world over, remember where and when they recently found food. A number of plants have nectar available at regularly scheduled times. Honeybees become familiar with the schedules of their favorite plants, and turn up promptly. If a pollinator takes all the available nectar from a flower, there is none for the next visitor. This may be a sign that the flower is sexually satisfied or worn out, in which case no more nectar is forthcoming, or the nectar builds up and flows again as the flower is once more ready for business. Some flowers have constant supplies at their peak of sexual maturity, but in order for cross-pollination to work, there has to be a tantalizing rationing system. A visitor never gets as much nectar as it would like because sated guests do not fly on to the next flower.

Drops of nectar can be seen oozing from inside crown imperial flowers.

Rob Proctor

FOOD FOR A COLD DAY

Dandelions are particularly successful plants because they produce nectar at lower temperatures than most flowers, so whenever it is chilly they can corner the market. At the end of winter, flowering snowdrops (*Galanthus*) and Christmas roses (*Helleborus niger*) make lots of nectar for the bees that are ready to get their hives into production again.

GLAMOROUS OR GAMIN

The small green or white flowers of plants like rock-foil (*Saxifraga* sp.), carrot (*Daucus carota*), donkey tail spurge (*Euphorbia myrsinites*) and grapes (*Vitis* sp.) are so small and unlovely it might seem they would never attract a partner. But these flowers do not need to be larger; their nectar is entirely exposed at the surface of the flower, easy to see, smell and feast on. They attract their own following of short-tongued bees and some flies and wasps.

Other flowers have partly hidden nectar with flowers that are often pretty, but not the major attraction of a garden. This group includes fruit trees such as plum (*Prunus*) and pear (*Pyrus*), strawberry (*Fragaria*), raspberry (*Rubus*), buttercups (*Ranunculus*) and many flowers in the mustard family (*Brassicaceae*). They draw such insects as bees, syrphid flies and some butterflies. The most glamorous and sweet smelling flowers usually have totally concealed nectar.

Top: Honeysuckle with concealed nectar
Bottom: Donkey tail spurge with exposed nectar

Pollen

Nectar offers pollinators fast food, but flowers need to provide something more sustaining for their visitors. Pollen is a major plant bribe and an excellent food source that contains protein and smaller quantities of starch, sugars, fat or oil, minerals, antioxidants, vitamins and free amino acids.

Pollen grains carry the plant's male genes, so no plant can afford to have them all consumed. Plants produce an abundance of pollen, so some of it can be eaten by insects and collected by bees and there is still a sufficient amount to be transferred to other flowers. Tibouchina, a tropical shrub with exotic purple flowers, has two kinds of pollen grains on separate anthers, purple ones for sex, yellow for food. A number of plants, including some penstemons and mulleins, have a similar advantage.

Flies and beetles eat some pollen, but bees are the major consumers and the only insects that collect and store it. Worker honeybees laboriously load up with pounds of pollen a year, feeding most of it to

Honeybee collecting pollen from sun roses

their young larvae in the hive. As the bees fly along they gather up the loose pollen on their bodies with their legs, but in spite of their industriousness there are often a few grains left somewhere on their heads or abdomen so there is still ample opportunity for sex to take place in the garden.

Like nectar, pollen is variable. Some of it is powdery and easily blown by the wind. As this is not always desirable, some plants have anthers that are pressed tightly together so pollen cannot be dispersed or collected until a proper pollinator comes along and pries them apart. Other pollen is viscous. Rhododendron pollen is easy for bees to gather as the grains stick together.

Bee flowers such as camellias, St.-John's-wort (*Hypericum*), begonias, clematis, roses and poppies offer no nectar; pollen is their only food bribe.

Right: The filaments of acanthus flowers are bent so the anthers face each other.
Bottom: The only reward a rose offers is pollen.

Other Rewards

Insects need shelter as well as food. Flowers have evolved to lure insects to them by providing an ideal place to spend some time clambering about, with each movement providing an added opportunity for exchanging pollen. Flowers supply insects with a place to rest, stay warm and hide from weather and predators. Male solitary bees, who don't have to rush home each evening, often sleep overnight in flowers. (Walk around your garden on a crisp fall morning and see how many bees have decided to sleep over.)

Index Stock

MEET A MATE

Promiscuous plants, with flowers that are ready to be pollinated by anything, can be like a busy singles' bar on a Friday night, full of people seeking a drink and a partner. Many insects can also expect to meet a member of the opposite sex in a flower, enjoy a meal together and find a place for the night.

Bees sleeping in a clematis. On chilly mornings they cannot be disturbed until the sun has warmed them sufficiently to enable them to fly.

70

GRAB A BITE

Predatory and beautifully camouflaged insects and spiders lie in wait in flowers and ambush smaller insects. Crab spiders change the color of their bodies to blend with the flower they are hiding in. Gardeners are used to seeing other spider webs in their flower beds, often carefully located to trap insects flying around flowers. Birds also seek insects in blossoms and may help pollinate the flowers as they peck about.

BREED

A few insects lay eggs in flowers, and many lay them on plant stems and foliage. Some flowers imitate an insect's normal breeding site, encouraging it to visit and reproduce. A particularly foul-smelling orchid, colored like rotting flesh, attracts carrion-eating flies to breed on it. But of course, if the fly larvae hatch, they soon starve to death.

HOME GOODS AND SEXUAL TURN-ONS

Besides nectar and pollen, honeybees gather propolis from some plants, a kind of glue used to seal the hive and make repairs, and also oils that are a nutritional supplement for their young. Aphrodisiacs make good insect bribes. As you can imagine, re-search in this area is difficult to conduct, and there is much more to be done. But it is known that some plants, particularly tropical ones, produce oils that insects spread on themselves in order to be more attractive to the opposite sex. Pass the flowers, please.

Top: Beetles consorting on blue mist spirea
Bottom: Bee gathering pollen in a prickly pear flower

71

5 PAIN AND SHAME

At some time or other we all have met charming people who we are shocked to discover have a criminal aspect. There is a group of plants like this, the arums and arisaemas being two examples, who lure pollinators to their bizarre flowers for their sexual needs, and then hold them captive, only releasing them at their convenience.

LORDS-AND-LADIES (*Arum maculatum*)

This plant is also called Adam-and-Eve, and these quaint old folk names could refer to the phallic appearance of the long spadix in the middle of the flower, surrounded by an enveloping sheath. However, the mission of the strange looking flowers of lords-and-ladies is their own fertilization. They lure dung flies and similar insects with a fetid smell, some warmth generated by the stiff, purple spadix, a false offer of shelter and a place to lay their eggs. The upper part of the spadix is full of starch that is actually burned by the flower to produce heat. This function uses up a lot of the plant's energy, but it must be effective or the plant wouldn't do it. Perhaps it makes the mimicry of warm flesh even more realistic, and helps disseminate the odor through the cool evening air.

Inside a chamber at the base of the spadix are many minute female flowers who start out mature and receptive. Small flies enter the lords-and-ladies through an opening fringed with downward facing hairs. Once inside they are trapped in a chamber, but can fly and crawl about, feed on nectar and if they have just arrived from a similar plant, may accidentally introduce some arum pollen and leave it on the stigmas, fertilizing the ovules. Then, with its female mission accomplished, the whole contraption enters its male phase. Hairs wither, allowing the flies to proceed up the spadix to another section of the chamber where there are many miniature male flowers with anthers that are now ready to shower newly arrived insects with pollen. Finally, the last guard hairs droop, and any prisoners who have not died are free to fly off and fertilize another lords-and-ladies.

There are many different kinds of arums. *Arum italicum* is widely grown in shady gardens for its handsome foliage, scarlet fruit and unusual flowers.

Panayoti Kelaidis

Lords-and-ladies

JACK-IN-THE-PULPIT (*Arisaema triphyllum*)

Arisaemas look somewhat like arums, with a long appendage sticking up inside a chamber, but with a flopped over hood. Presumably this is "Jack" standing in his pulpit. This picturesque perennial often has separate male and female plants, so some of the "Jacks" are "Jills." In the evenings, gnats gather around the male plant's flower, fall into the prison, whine around getting covered with pollen and then escape through a special hole.

Female plants attract gnats similarly. Some may bring pollen after they have visited the male plant, but these gnats are doomed for when they are ready to leave there is no exit and they are sacrificed to the cause of fertilization.

Above: Jack-in-the-pulpit
Top right: Mouse plant

MOUSE PLANT (*Arisarum proboscideum*)

Are flies attracted to this plant by the funguslike smell, or the resemblance to mice, with stinking, long, bare tails? Either way it is yet another plant like the arums and arisaemas that lures small insects with its shape, warmth and foul smells into traplike chambers, where they are expected to fertilize the plant's sexual organs before perhaps being allowed to leave.

Eating the Victims

The pitcher plant (*Sarracenia* sp.), sundew (*Drosera*) and well-known venus's flytrap (*Dionaea muscipula*) have flowers that attract pollinating insects. These menacing plants also sport modified leaves with specialized mechanisms for catching and digesting their guests. They flourish in Florida and other places with warm, wet, boggy areas where plants cannot draw up sufficient nutrients through their roots so they trap and absorb proteins and other substances from insects. These are possibly the same insects that have just fertilized their flowers.

Murder Most Foul

ELEPHANT EAR (*Alocasia* sp.)
Gardeners dread slugs and snails with good reason, as they damage far more plants than they help. These mollusks' tongues are rough, like sandpaper, with thousands of minute teeth that can ruin both leaves and petals. Slugs prefer damp locations with fresh young plant shoots or smelly, decomposing vegetation. The bold flowers of elephant's ear plant (*Alocasia* sp.) actually encourage snails to pollinate them by a sinister sequence of events. The flower gives off a decaying smell to seduce the snails with a promise of food. When a snail enters the funnel-shaped chamber of a flower in its male phase it gets covered with pollen but finds nothing to eat. Trying another flower, it slowly eases its slimy way down to the female parts and starts eating. The flower reacts by releasing a burning chemical (calcium oxalate crystals), and the snail writhes in pain, smearing the pollen on its body around, fertilizing the flower in its agony. It may never visit another *Alocasia*, but that particular plant's future is assured. Few plants deal with slugs and snails so succinctly, and they are very minor pollinators. There are gardeners who would envy the elephant ear's success.

Left: Elephant ear foliage
Right: Pitcher plant

BUTTERFLY FLOWER (*Asclepias tuberosa*)

We like to think of flowers as innocent, but plants that have not strived ferociously to survive died long ago. The butterfly flower is a favorite garden perennial with a dazzling yet dangerous display. The complex flowers have five nectaries that entice many insects, including bees and butterflies. When insects stand on the flower mechanism and drink at the cups of nectar their legs sometimes slip into slots in the stamens. Instead of powdery pollen, butterfly flowers have a pair of sticky balls of pollen grains joined by a slender thread. These pollinia adhere to the intruding insect limb or tongue and when the insect flies off to the next flower they may be poked into similar slots, pushing the pollen against the concealed part of the stigma and fertilizing the flower.

Butterfly flowers are traps for the weak and unwary, however. Occasionally insects' legs or butterflies' tongues are stuck in the slots, and unless they are strong enough to pull free they are snared until they die. The flower, oblivious to the murder, sets about reproducing itself. In turn the Asclepias flowers are helpless if not pollinated by a visiting insect, since they cannot self-fertilize and will bloom for days while waiting for a partner (or victim).

Povy Kendal Atchison

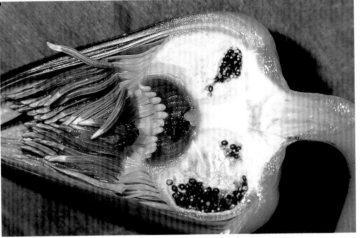

Dissection by Dr. Nancy Style/Povy Kendal Atchisonr

WATER LILIES (*Nymphaea*)

Water lilies are so lovely that it is hard to believe that some of them can be accused of murder for sex. When a day-flowering water lily first opens it is a female with a receptive stigma. The fragrant perfume attracts a host of insects, some of whom arrive with pollen from other water lilies, but they often slide into the bottom of the slippery flower and drown in a pool of liquid nectar surrounding the stigma. This water lily closes at night and opens the next day in its male phase. The stamens lengthen and form a platform above the liquid on which more insects land and get covered with pollen, then they are free to fly off to another young water lily and another chance of drowning.

Left: Monarch butterfly with a butterfly flower
Top: First and second day flower of a waterlily.
Bottom: Dissected waterlily showing captured insects

Robert Heapes

75

Fraudulent Advertisements and Pseudo-Copulation

We have all been "had" by advertising come-ons, and it is little help to know that insects are just as gullible as we are. The thousands of orchid species have evolved to fool all of us, cloaking their sexual urgency with sophisticated shapes and techniques so they are rarely what they appear to be. They are a diverse family of flowers, with each kind pollinated by particular insects on whom they are completely dependent. Most orchids cannot self-fertilize, so they may bloom for a long time while waiting for their partner. Some orchids bribe pollinators with nectar. Ophrys orchids and others mimic a female insect, usually a bee or wasp, luring males with odors of females ready for sex, petal patterns that are passable forgeries of females and textures that stimulate the male sexual organs. Botanists call it pseudo-copulation. It may be pseudo for the bee, but the sex is real for the orchid, as it either accepts delivery of pollen from another flower or deposits pollen for delivery on a lecherous insect. The insect thinks, at least temporarily, that it has found a willing partner and makes energetic copulation movements. The ruse works best, however, if the insect is not completely satisfied, for then it flies off enthusiastically to the next likely looking orchid. There is a species of oncidium orchid, equally full of duplicity, whose flowers flutter in a breeze so they look like certain male bees. This provokes other bees to protect their territory by attacking, thereby fertilizing the orchid as they go after one flower then another. It is easy to feel sorry for all the insects that are duped and hypnotized by orchids, but there are a variety of compensations. Besides pseudo-sex and nectar, some orchids offer tasty imitation pollen on their lower lips that encourage bee visits, and erotic scents and oils that insects collect for their own courtship.

The male and female parts of orchids are not long-stemmed, as in many flowers, but appear as stubs welded onto a single column. A pair of waxy blobs of pollen, or pollinia, are deposited on the lusty suitors with all sorts of masterly deceptions that exploit either or both sexes of insects. Each orchid flower has only one set of pollinia, so the transfer has to be very precise, or the single chance is lost.

The majority of wild orchids grow in remote tropical areas, not in American gardens, and therefore few of their pollinators live here either. Since many orchids will cross-pollinate readily with another, species growers around the world are intervening, playing pseudo-insect and breeding new orchid hybrids each year.

Right top: Oncidium henekenii is an orchid that is pollinated when male bees try to mate with the flower, which resembles a female bee.
Right bottom: This South American orchid (Trichoceros antennifera) fools a species of fly.
Far right: Male Eucera bees are lured by this Ophrys fuciflora orchid's similarity to a female bee.

6 INTIMATE PARTNERS

Bees Do It

Most insects have close relationships with plants, living in and feeding on either live or dead plant material. Bees are special, however, and are the most beneficial insect for gardens and gardeners. The thousands of species of bees can be divided into two kinds: social bees who live in domestic or wild colonies, and solitary bees who live mostly alone. The lives of flowering plants and bees are intimately connected, but they exploit each other shamelessly. In turn humans use bees as unwitting partners. In many parts of the world domesticated honeybees (*Apis mellifera*) are critical to gardeners and agriculture. They pollinate plants as they collect food from masses of flowers every warm day in order to feed their colony and store honey for the winter. They are the only insects whose energies we harness for food, pollination and profit. In temperate climates other kinds of bees don't feed a colony year round, so they make fewer flower visits and less honey.

HONEYBEES

Honeybees live in a rigid, complex society. A beehive may contain more than 50,000 bees. Each performs a role and, by human standards, performs its task diligently until it dies. A colony usually has one adult queen who lays eggs all spring and summer while being fed and waited on by worker bees inside the hive. The male bees' (drones) only job is to mate with the queen. Only the fittest succeed, assuring a healthy new batch of bees. Nearly all of the bees in a colony or hive are virgin female workers. Drugged by the pheromones of the queen into compliance, and ignored by the drones due to their immature ovaries and lack of sex appeal, some of these female bees work themselves to death in about six weeks. The queen bees' eggs hatch into grublike larvae that grow rapidly in their cells until they pupate, a quiescent state during which they metamorphose into young adult bees.

A selection of garden bee flowers

Rob Proctor

OUTDOOR BEES

The honeybees that we see in our gardens are workers assigned to either scout for flowers or forage for nectar and honey. Scout workers leave the hive early in the morning. They can be seen flying around, checking briefly on the status of newly opened flowers. When they find suitable blooms they return to the hive and perform dancelike steps while communicating the location and smell of the flowers to foraging bees.

Foraging bees become familiar with the color, smell and structure of certain flowers. With a little practice they become very efficient at collecting from them. Once they have found a good source of food, they retain loyalty to that type of flower and keep collecting from it as long as the supply lasts.

BEE GATHERING

Bees tend to stop only briefly at each flower to gather food. When honeybees collect nectar they often climb on or into a flower and grip on with some of their six legs. They push a tube containing their medium length tongues (about one quarter inch in length) into the flower nectaries and draw up the liquid. The worker uses some of the nectar for his own energy and the rest is stored in the nectar stomach.

While gathering pollen, bees can be observed in the garden scuttling around the open bowls of flowers, such as anemones, roses and poppies, collecting pollen with the front legs, pushing it to the back legs, and stashing it away in what are called baskets. Bees only carry little baskets in fairy stories. The back pair of legs on a foraging bee has a concave area and branched hairs at angles that look like baskets when full of yellow pollen. As with everything about flowers and bees, there are many different adaptations. The hind leg hair arrangement varies with the type of pollen the bee usually gathers. Bees who tend to visit flowers with powdery pollen have tightly woven baskets, and those who collect from flowers with sticky pollen have loosely woven ones. Bees also have "combs" on their legs that they pull across their bodies, gathering up loose flower pollen, and then pack it into the baskets. Meanwhile, although the bees are said to be oblivious to the procreative act they may have performed for the plants, their visits from flower to flower have ensured future plants for new generations of bees, and these plants will ensure that those bees can feed their young and have enough left over to see them through other winters. Call them intimate partnerships.

BACK HOME

Honeybees are conscientious workers. When they have a load they don't dally but fly in a "beeline" back to their hive. If you see a bee flying in a straight line it is probably on its way home. They can carry almost their own weight, and sometimes look so laden they can hardly take off. Never wasting a moment they continue to pack pollen into the baskets as they fly along. Back at the hive the pollen is unloaded from the baskets and set aside for the manufacture of "bee bread." Nectar is regurgitated and stored in honey combs. When the honey is ready, bees cover the full cells with wax. Honeybees have glands inside their bodies that can change some of the nectar into liquid wax that is secreted from underneath their bodies, hardens in the air, and is pried off with spurs on their legs. All this work has to be exhausting. But the queen bee keeps laying eggs during the warm months so new larvae are constantly growing to replace worn-out workers. Newly hatched female adults learn their tasks from older workers. The fortunate ones get to forage in people's gardens.

Honey Bees Love Blue and Yellow Flowers

Top: Penstemon and iris
Bottom: Dahlia

big woolly bumblebees are native North Americans. They are excellent flower pollinators for several reasons: their hairy bodies collect quantities of pollen, they are strong enough to force their way into many flowers and they can carry a large load of pollen in their baskets. In addition, theirtongues are longer than most bees, which enables them to reach farther into flowers. Finally, they can forage at higher altitudes, in colder places and at colder times than other insects.

Bumblebees also have the unique ability of making some flowers emit clouds of ripe, powdery pollen by vibrating their muscles, which jiggles the flower to a particular resonance. Some native flowers are programmed to only dispense pollen when vibrated by a bumblebee. (Honeybees cannot do it.) This adaptation gives the bumblebee a monopoly on the flower, the plant a reliable cross-pollinator and it prevents the pollen being dispersed by a fickle wind.

BUMBLING HOME

In North America bumblebees live either alone or in small colonies of up to 400. The queen usually mates in the fall, hibernates in the winter and lays eggs in an old mouse nest, or similar grassy place, in the spring. She starts out by doing all the work herself, building wax cells and collecting nectar and pollen. When young adult bees emerge they take over the flower visiting so the queen can keep laying.

Bumblebees do not communicate by dancing like honeybees, and they forage in many flowers. But plump, tubular flowers such as foxgloves, large penstemons and campanulas are well adapted to bumblebees and are bumble favorites. Bumblebees will not be tamed. They dislike being moved and

BUMBLEBEES: BUMBLING SEX

Before honeybees were introduced into North America from Europe much of the flowering plant pollinating was performed by other kinds of bees. They are still important, particularly to the native wildflowers that so many of us are growing in our gardens, and to other garden flowers to which the bees have become adapted. Some

Bumblebee visiting clary sage

thrive on undisturbed land. These wild, free-spirited bees should be encouraged in the garden. Many gardeners will empathize with them.

OTHER WILD BEES

There are hundreds of different kinds of lesser known bees in North America. Each bee's life cycle is synchronized with certain sorts of flowers and they will only emerge when "their" flowers are in bloom. One such species is the leaf cutter bees, who cut pieces out of leaves to create their nests. They particularly like roses. Gardeners may find coin-sized holes in their rose leaves, evidence of leaf cutter theft, but the damage is not usually critical and the free pollination is a gift in exchange.

ROBBER BEES

There are times when bees do not want to stick their heads in flowers and get thumped by exploding

stamens and covered with pollen, so the bees bite holes in the sides of tubular flowers, reaching the nectar without offering a sexual payback. It is a disaster for the plant. The robber bees steal the nectar and other insects use the hole, increasing the damage.

Top: Marigolds
Bottom: Azaleas

Wasps ...
Getting Waspish

People dislike wasps, especially in their gardens, for several reasons. Wasps are not nearly as useful as bees. In temperate climates they are summer insects and are not around to pollinate spring flowers. Unlike bees, wasps eat a wide range of foods. They use their strong jaws to kill spiders and insects, including bees, which they feed to their larvae as protein. Wasps love sweet substances too; they bite into ripe fruit and visit flowers for nectar. The body hairs on wasps are sleeker than those of bees, so although wasps are pollinators, the pollen does not cling to them so readily and is not transferred to flowers so reliably.

Because they like meat, wasps favor some of the dingier colored flowers, and they do not delve deeply into blooms. Flowers such as helleborines (*Epipactis*) and some of the maroon or dusky penstemons are perfect partners for wasps.

Left: Bumblebee on tithonia
Top: Nectaroscordum siculum
Bottom: Dusky penstemon

*Dead wasps are the only wasps
some people want in their gardens.*

85

Butterflies ... Fluttering About

Gardeners love butterflies posing picturesquely on their flowers. Butterfly gardens are in vogue and shrubs, perennials and annuals that promise to entice these beautiful insects are much sought after. More butterflies mean more caterpillars, but hold the insecticide, it also means more pollination for flowers.

Butterflies have several characteristics that make them particularly well suited to be plant partners in a garden. They love a sunny, sheltered place where they can fly and feed on nectar during the day. Butterflies can see colors and have an excellent sense of smell, gathering information with a pair of sensitive antennae. They need to land before feeding, and prefer flat-topped flowers in an open location. They have thin, hollow tongues, at least as long as their bodies, enabling them to reach deeply into flowers. The tongues unroll to feed and roll up when not in use.

Right: A garden of butterfly flowers and swallowtail butterfly
Left: Some more of the summer flowers butterflies love

Birds eat butterflies, so they have to be constantly alert. Fluttering about may make them hard to catch, but they are too wary to feed under leaves or inside bell-shaped flowers where they cannot look around. Butterflies will often feed on flowers that are similar in color to themselves, providing instant camouflage, and they rest their wings upright, making them less obvious to predators.

Top: This butterfly is camouflaged as it feeds from the flowers of Maltese cross.
Left: A butterfly unrolling its tongue ready to plunge it into the depths of a lantana blossom

Flowers Butterflies Love

Butterflies like the fresh scent of newly opened flowers. They favor hot colors, but can be found on flowers of every hue. They have a reputation for not being very clever, and it is true that many butterfly flowers have grooves that guide the long tongues down to the nectar.

Colorful garden flowers that entice butterflies include bright composites such as zinnias (*Zinnia*), Mexican sunflowers (*Tithonia*), pot marigolds (*Calendula*) and tickseed (*Bidens aristosa*); many inflorescences of tiny, bunched flowers such as butterfly bush (*Buddleia*), butterfly flower (*Asclepias*), blazing star (*Liatris* sp.), bee balm (*Monarda*) and verbena (*Verbena* sp.); garden flowers with long, narrow tubular flowers (too narrow for a bee to climb into), and with petals flared out at the front so butterflies can land to feed, such as tobacco flowers (*Nicotiana*), phlox and impatiens; and finally several of the flowering herbs like mints (*Mentha*) and hyssops (*Agastache*).

Arching verbenas provide a perfect landing platform for butterflies.

Enchanted Evenings ... Moths

Who wants a moth in their garden? Not many people. Moths are equated with holes in clothes and do not have the romantic image of butterflies. This may be somewhat unfair. A garden on a hot summer night, full of pale fragrant flowers and pale, fluffy moths can be a sexy place. Nectar-sipping moths are excellent plant pollinators.

The main difference between American moths and butterflies is that, although a few are active in the daytime, most moths are nocturnal. They tend to be fat and hairy, with feathery antennae, to hover while feeding, and rest with their wings horizontal.

Plants that bribe moths to perform their pollination have a number of things in common, including: opening at dusk and staying open all night, oozing plenty of nectar, gleaming in the dark with white or pastel coloring and smelling sweetly, sometimes with stripes of scent leading past their sexual parts to the nectaries. They include such garden flowers as some evening primroses (*Oenothera*), Jimsonweed (*Datura*), some tobacco plants (*Nicotiana*) and some honeysuckles (*Lonicera*).

Top: This evening primrose is typical of flowers that moths frequent.
Left: Garden plants that are partners with moths

Rob Proctor

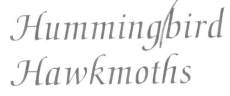

Moth illustration by Frances C. Mishler

Hummingbird Hawkmoths

There are many kinds of hawkmoths but one in particular really gets a plant's and gardener's attention. These moths mimic hummingbirds so cleverly that at a distance they are hard to distinguish from the real thing. Predators find hummingbirds unappetizing, so looking like one is an effective way for a moth to protect itself.

Hummingbird hawkmoths' appearance—rapid beating of wings and habit of darting forward into a flower and reversing back out again—are a creditable piece of acting. These hawkmoths even feed during the afternoon and favor brilliantly colored trumpet-shaped flowers like nasturtiums, exactly as hummingbirds do.

Left: Hummingbird hawkmoth feeding at the open mouth of the nasturtiums

Flies ... Scraping the Bottom of the Market

From an aesthetic point of view some flies are repulsive. Many breed on excrement, and frequent rotting dead animal or vegetable matter. As children we were always told that flies never washed their hands or feet. I don't know if this is true, but you get the picture. It is hard to imagine anything taking advantage of this situation, but some flowers do.

Certain plants attract flies by having flowers that are dung-colored, damp, dark and smelly. In the competitive plant world it is a different niche, a specialized market that appeals to some flies and even some mosquitoes and beetles.

FOUL-SMELLING GARDEN FLOWERS THAT ATTRACT FLIES

Dreary colors and putrid smells are not appealing to the average gardener, but some fly-partner plants, such as wild ginger (*Asarum canadense*), are grown for their beautiful foliage, and their unusual flowers are hardly noticed. Not all flies eat nectar or pollen. Some are lured to flowers by the stench, and are looking for other food or a place to lay eggs. Some of these flowers mimic animals by having a hairy orifice.

Selling something by drawing a crowd is an old marketing trick, and flowers do it too. Spotted patterns on petals may mimic a cluster of flies feeding, attracting even more flies. Flowers that entice such flies are often low to the ground, purplish or brown colored, with spots or mottling. Some have an opening that flies can crawl into and a chamber large enough for several flies at once.

Rob Proctor

Flowers with nectar that flies favor

Sweet Fly-Flowers

What are to us much nicer kinds of flies feed on both pollen and nectar. They have long tongues and particularly favor the composite flowers that have a flat surface facing up toward the sun, and tiny florets scaled down to the small size of many flies. Flies do not like to fly up into hanging bell-shaped flowers.

Other types of flies prefer nectar that is visible, not concealed as in composites, so some fly-flowers are diminutive, pastel or pale greenish colored. Again they are often plants that are admired in the garden for their foliage.

The last group of garden plants that use flies as pollinators have small tubular flowers. They include forget-me-not (*Myosotis*), sea lavender (*Limonium*), thyme (*Thymus*), good-luck plant (*Oxalis*), lungwort (*Pulmonaria*), lesser periwinkle (*Vinca minor*) and primrose (*Primula*).

It is hard to imagine a world without flies. They are such a huge and successful family of insects that it is not surprising that hundreds of flowers all over the world have adapted and evolved to please and use these insects who never seem to be in short supply. The effort of producing a flower large and appealing enough for a bee, bird or bat is considerable. Growing little flowers, with small amounts of nectar to attract homely little flies to perform the same sex is an efficient strategy in an uncertain world.

Top: Iceland poppy
Second: Crambe
Third: Snow-in-summer
Bottom: Dogwood

Old Reliables ... Beetles

Fossil records show that beetles are one of the oldest forms of insects. Some beetles have prospered so well that they have not needed to change much since the dawn of flowers. They count on a hard exterior to protect them from predators. Instead of escaping by flying away, like butterflies, beetles can stay in a flower for a long time, ambling about, eating, resting or even mating with another beetle.

Most beetles cannot perceive color, just shades of light and dark, so the flowers they visit are often white. Beetle flowers are also strong so they can survive rough handling, and their ovaries are usually underneath the flower so voracious beetles are less likely to devour them. Beetles have a good sense of smell, and their flowers are scented. Some beetles are scavengers, eating decaying matter, and they can be found in flowers that imitate these environments.

Other beetles are pollen eaters, and flowers that rely on them for pollination tend to have sticky pollen that clings briefly to the shiny beetles as they feed and is transferred to female flower parts as the beetle stumbles over other blooms. Flowers such as potatoes (*Solanum*), elderberry (*Sambucus*), poppies (*Papaver*) and roses (*Rosa*) produce an abundance of pollen that attract small beetles.

Yet a different sort of beetle drinks nectar, and some species have specially adapted mouth parts so they can lap it up. The ancient order of beetles may not be as intelligent or sophisticated as some more recently evolved insects, but the fact that they have survived for millennia shows how successful they are and what reliable partners they make for some flowers.

Left: Rose malva   Right: Yarrow

Potential Pain ... Ants

Top: *Zinnia*
Bottom: *Allium*

A few flowers have relationships with ants, but ants can be destructive to flowers and are rarely used as pollinators. Instead they are used by plants as guards and rewarded with nectar. Ants love nectar, and it is collected by wingless workers. Like bees, they are social insects and live in elaborately constructed and organized colonies, nurturing their young.

Some plants take advantage of the ant's need for nectar by growing special nectaries, well away from the sexual organs but available to worker ants. Some of the vetches (*Vicia*) have theses nectaries in leaf stipules, while cherry laurels (*Prunus laureocerasus*) have them on their leaf blades, making them sticky. In turn, ants fiercely guard their source of food by biting and stinging, discouraging robber bees and other insects who steal nectar without pollinating the flower.

Other plants have evolved with barriers to prevent destructive ants from reaching their flowers. Sometimes the barriers take the form of paired leaves opposite each other along the stem, joined in the middle to collect rain or dew, making a watery obstruction that the ants cannot circumvent. Other plants have sticky stems that prevent ants from climbing them.

A few low growing plants with tiny inconspicuous flowers, and without enough nectar for bees, are adapted to permit ants to extract nectar in return for pollination. These plants thrive in the desert where worker ants climb from flower to flower, fortuitously transferring pollen. Flying insects do the same work much more effectively.

Sex Is for the Birds

It has taken thousands of years for some plants to learn how to lure birds to perform their sexual needs. A few birds have also adapted to using flowers as a major food source. Together these plants and birds have evolved to suit each other, growing in a distinctive way that makes the flowers different from the insect-pollinated species, and the birds different from, for example, the seed or berry eaters.

HUMMINGBIRDS

Hummingbirds feed on sugary nectar and protein-rich insects to fuel their extremely high metabolic rate. They need to consume about half their weight in food every day, so must spend their lives close to a supply of blooming plants. Nearly all of the 300 or so species are natives of South or Central America, and just a few of them migrate north each spring, following the sequence of opening flowers into North America. Hummingbirds have almost no sense of smell and identify the flowers they need firstly by their bright color, preferring red. Anyone who attracts hummingbirds to a feeder in their garden knows that as long as parts of the feeder are red they will try and use it.

Hummingbirds feed in flight and have the ability to fly in any direction, including backwards. This makes it easy for them to fly up into a flower, thrust their beak to the back, spending about one and a half seconds licking up nectar with their very long tongue before reversing out, dropping down and flying diagonally up into the next flower.

Left: Hummingbird flowers

Rob Proctor

Flowers that appeal to hummingbirds visiting North America usually have the following characteristics: they flower in summer during the daytime, have plenty of nectar and a bright red color, although other hot colors ar perused. The flowers have no scent and no landing area, and face outward or downward, with a clear area for the birds' flying approach. The flowers also need to be fairly strong to be able to withstand repeated bird visits, medium to large sized and open for several days.

Left: Broadbill hummingbird feeding at claret cup cactus
Right: Montbretia

Flowers Adapted to Hummingbirds

Red, tubular garden flowers pollinated by hummingbirds include:

California fuchsia (*Zauschneria californica*)
trumpet honeysuckle (*Lonicera sempervirens*)
beard tongue (*Penstemon barbatus* and *P. eatonii*)
red-hot-poker (*kniphofia uvaria*)
trumpet vine (*Campsis radicans*)
montbretia (*Crocosmia*)
scarlet gilia (*Ipomopsis aggregata*)
sages (*Salvia guaranitica, S.elegans, S. greggii*)
flaming trumpet (*Pyrostegia venusta*)
cape honeysuckle (*Tecomaria capensis*)

The following hummingbird flowers are all native to the Americas. They exclude bees and wasps by hiding nectar at the end of long, narrow spurs.

red columbine (*Aquilegia canadensis*)
nasturtium (*Tropaeolum*)
red delphinium (*Delphinium cardinale*)
jewelweed (*Impatiens capensis*)

*Left: A gold finch on a red-hot-poker
in the author's garden
Right: Columbine*

There are other red garden flowers that lure hummingbirds to nestle up to the flowers' pollen and pistils with a bribe of nectar, but these flowers don't have bee-excluding features such as narrow tubular blooms or spurs. They include:

cardinal flower (*Lobelia cardinalis*)
Oswego tea or bee balm (*Monarda didyma*)
ladies'-teardrops (*Fuchsia*)
trailing lantana (*lantana montevidensis*)
cardinal climber (*Ipomoea quamoclit*)
shrimp plant (*Justicia brandegeana*)
Chinese hibiscus (*Hibiscus rosa-sinensis*)
scarlet monkey flower (*Mimulus cardinalis*)
bougainvillea (*Bougainvillea*)
coral bells (*Heuchera*)

Male hummingbirds are territorial and defend their air space fiercely from rival males. This trait can be detrimental to flowers that need cross-pollination, but by limiting a hummingbird's flight area it ensures flowers multiple visits, giving each bloom more opportunities to be pollinated at just the right moment. Gardeners can encourage hummingbirds to breed by planting passionate red flowers that have a carnal relationship with these dashing aviators.

Penstemons

Other Things Pollinate Too

In North America other small birds will visit flowers too. For example, some finches not only enjoy drinking from a garden hummingbird feeder, but they can also be seen visiting the bright waxy flowers of red-hot-pokers. Many birds search for insects in flowers and adjacent dead flower heads for seeds. Any of these visits may facilitate cross-pollination for the plant, but they are additional chances, rather than the primary source.

There are no wild hummingbirds in Europe or in Asia north of the Himalayas, but tropical and subtropical regions have many plants with blooms sturdy enough for other bird encounters, and some provide a virtual feast of nectar and pollen washed down with accumulated rainwater. The large blue and orange bird-of-paradise flowers (*Strelitzia reginae*) are often used in American flower arrangements. They have an intriguing mechanism triggered by birds in their native South Africa. To feed on the nectar in the orange part of the flower, the bird must perch on a blue petal segment hiding the sexual organs. These are exposed when the weight of the bird allows them to rear up, dusting pollen on the feathered belly, ready for transfer to the next *Strelitzia*.

Some of the Australian banksia flowers and South African proteas are pollinated by birds and small mammals such as possums. They have bunches of large stamens that stick up like a brush. These hardy flowers last for weeks, and are a favorite of American florists.

John Stone, Australia (both photos)

Left: Australian honey possum on claw flower
Bottom: New Holland honey eater on Australian showy banksia

Sex in the 'Dark … 'Bats

Just the thought of touching bats alarms some of us. We equate bats with Halloween and witches, not with gorgeous flowers and sex. However, in the hot, dry deserts of the southwestern United States, migrating bats from Mexico pollinate cactus flowers as they feast on nectar. Later in the summer, they eat the fruit of the same plants and help disperse the seeds, completing the reproductive cycle. One can hardly get more intimate than that.

Bats fly and feed at night. They have very poor eyesight and color sense and rely on their acute sense of smell to find suitable flowers. Bats also feed in flight. As they press their furry heads deep into large flowers the bats become smothered with floury pollen. They use their long tongues to lick some of the pollen off their eyes, ears and noses, but plenty remains to be transferred to the next flower.

As bat partners, some cacti have evolved with big, strong, pale-colored flowers that open at night and smell powerful at the time the Mexican bats are migrating through. They produce great quantities of nectar and pollen, and their extended female parts are flexible enough to withstand the weight of a bat without snapping off. The giant saguaro, organ pipe and cardoon cacti are all pollinated by Mexican bats and have flowers that are open at night. The flowers may still be open part of the next day, however, to give birds and bees a chance to visit too. If none of this works, the cactus may self-pollinate. Cacti need to keep many options open in the harsh desert environment. As the bats migrate back to Mexico in the fall they seek out agave flowers, feeding on their nectar and pollinating them. Sadly, the Mexican bats,

the cacti and the agaves all seem to be disappearing from the wild in parts of the Southwest. Garden specimens should be nurtured and, of course, never dug up from the desert.

Bat feeding on cactus

D. Tuttle, Bat Conservation Society

7 BLOWN AWAY BY THE WIND

There are many plants that do not rely on insects or any animals for pollination but let the wind perform their sex for them. This has a couple of advantages. First, the wind does not care what the plant looks like, nor does it need rewards for its services, so wind-pollinated plants do not have to expend energy manufacturing attractive petals, enticing perfumes or delicious nectar. Second, there is no waiting for the right pollinator. As long as there is a breeze, sex can take place 24 hours a day. The disadvantage of counting on the wind to disperse pollen is that there is no guarantee that any of it will arrive at the right place, so vast quantities of pollen are dispersed to increase the chances that at least one male pollen grain will land on a female receptive stigma.

Few wind-pollinated plants thrive in dense tropical jungles where there are thousands of different plant species growing close together and plenty of insects to fertilize flowers year round. Wind pollination works best in cold and temperate climates where plants in their natural habitat tend to grow in groups and pollen is blown from one plant to the other with some chance of success. The winters kill off many insects, so in early spring many deciduous trees, such as maples, oaks and beeches, bloom with insignificant little flowers before too many leaves are out to interfere with blowing pollen. Northern gardeners grow wind-pollinated trees, shrubs and grasses for their structural beauty and foliage rather than for their flowers. In the summer many grasses bloom and the wind blows their pollen unimpeded across open countryside and temperate grasslands. Seashore plants are often wind-pollinated. Gales and gusts make it hard for insects to fly about and a number of coastal plants have evolved with tiny flowers whose pollen is blown along the beaches.

In the wild, trees of the same species often grow in groves, facilitating cross-pollination from tree to tree. For instance, pollen is easily transferred by wind in a whole forest of lodgepole pines. Conifers such as pines produce pounds of powdery pollen that is blown around in yellow clouds. In mid-summer it can be swept up in the streets of towns near pine forests, and floats on lakes creating yellow waves. But gardeners usually don't want to raise a lot of tree seedlings, so planting just one of a species works well.

HOW THEY DO IT

Many wind-pollinated plants consist of unadorned sexual parts because beautiful petals could get in the way of pollen. Stigmas may be sticky and/or have a large surface area of feathery material, ensuring that the pollen that has landed does not get blown away again before it has had an opportunity to grow a pollen tube down to the ovary. The stamens have thin filaments that are easily jostled by a breeze.

There are different combinations of sexual orientation in wind-pollinated plants, just as there are in plants pollinated by animals and insects. Most

garden grasses and rushes are hermaphrodites; because the male and female organs are so close together these plants have either chemical or physical barriers to prevent self-fertilization. However, some grasses "self" and, if the parts are conveniently adjacent, it takes only a puff of wind to shake the pollen from the anthers to the stigma right next to it. Wind-pollinated garden

trees as spruce (*Picea*), pine (*Picus*), alder (*Alnus*), walnut (*Juglans*), oak (*Quercus*) and beech (*Fagus*) are in another category. They have separate male and female flowers growing on the same plant, while garden trees, such as poplar (*Populus*), yew (*Taxus*) and juniper (*Juniperus*), have male flowers on one tree and female flowers on another. It takes two plants, one of each sex, for the fertilization to occur.

Flowers pollinated by insects and birds may have the luxury of repeated visits, and many ovules capable of growing into seeds in each ovary. Such success is remote for wind-pollinated flowers. To improve their chances, the tough little blossoms usually last several days, and most have just one ovule in each ovary, like an oak's acorn.

Left: Water birch (Betula occidentalis) has tiny male, petalless flowers grouped into catkins, which are long dangling organs that dance in the wind, flinging their pollen into the air. The river birch's female flowers grow lower down the twigs, ready to catch a grain of male pollen. This may come from another tree or the catkin right above it.
Top: Wind pollinated garden plants

Rob Proctor

103

Having It Both Ways

Some plants are partly wind- and partly insect-pollinated. This may be because they are still evolving and are still adapted to a pollinator they used thousands of years ago. Rushes are thought to have been insect-pollinated in times past but are now mostly wind-pollinated. Garden plants, such as meadow rue (*Thalictrum*), and trees, such as linden (*Tilia*), are plants that are considered to be switching over, and are currently pollinated by both wind and insects. Both have small flowers, marginally attractive to insects, but with extended stamens that take advantage of the wind as well. The pollen of male willows (*Salix*) is both blown by the wind and collected by bees. Garden plants, such as snakeweed (*Polygonum bistorta*) and Himalayan border jewel (*Polygonum affine*), a native of rugged mountainsides, are designed to be pollinated by insects, if they are available, or by the wind in poor weather.

Left: Meadow rue
Middle: Willow
Right: Himalayan border jewel

A chestnut in flower in New Zealand. They are partly wind- and partly insect-pollinated.

Blown All Over

Most pollen is blown just a short distance, maybe a few inches or several yards. But some pollen is carried on air currents up to high altitudes, even into the jet stream, where it can travel for thousands of miles. At high altitudes, however, ultraviolet light damages pollen, and some species may not be viable more than a few hours. The recently discovered hole in the Earth's ozone layer lets in more ultraviolet light. It is not only harmful to humans but may injure some pollen too. Scientists have estimated that there are millions of grains of pollen on every square yard of earth. Windblown pollen has even been found in the middle of the Atlantic Ocean.

8 HUMAN INTERVENTION

People have been manipulating the sex lives of animals and plants to suit their needs for several thousand years, but recently the pace has picked up dramatically. On farms and in laboratories worldwide, artificial insemination and gene manipulation have become commonplace, driven by the pressures to produce marketable products that suit consumers' tastes and fashions. Garden trees, shrubs, bulbs, perennials and vegetables are all undergoing

transformations. Flower seed companies specializing in annuals and cut flowers have blossomed into global corporations with year-round operations.

The garden seed industry is structured in a series of steps starting with the selection and genetic engineering of plants at seed companies, who sell to brokers, who sell to plant growers or seed packagers, who supply retail outlets that purchase to please the rest of us. America's top-selling flowering annuals are currently impatiens, petunias, geraniums and marigolds. These and other popular plants such as pansies, primulas, snapdragons, cyclamens, dianthus and zinnias are constantly being improved by what is known as hybridizing.

Hybrid plants are the result of pollinating two distinctly different members of the same species. The seeds from this cross-pollination are called F1 hybrids, and plants produced from these seeds can incorporate the best characteristics of both parents, including hybrid vigor, uniformity and improved resistance to disease and insect damage. The second generations of plants, however, may not breed "true," and in order to retain the hybrids' desirable qualities, one must return to the parental lines.

Creating hybrids is a long-term investment, because it takes an average of eight years to make a hybrid annual—from the conception of the idea to full-scale production. Goldsmith Seeds, one of California's highly-regarded seed producers, takes the following steps to bring out a new garden annual. First, research staff gather input from home gardeners and professional growers to set new flower breeding goals. Second, parent plants are selected from carefully-guarded collections of genetic lines, from wild types of university material for cross-pollination. Offspring of these parents are further inbred until there are populations of "true," or nearly identical plants which scientists use to make test crosses to select new breeding lines. The breeder uses a trained eye, intuition, a solid background in genetics, plus a little luck in deciding which parent lines will be put together in a hybrid cross. Flower size, petal shape and margin are just a few of the sought-after qualities. Breeders also cross-pollinate to produce new colors within a "series" of plants. For

Mac Hartshorn

Glamorous plants and people reflect human priorities.

example, a blue and red flowered plant may be crossed to produce a purple flowering one. Once a flowering series is established, different colors can be produced in a year or two. These may be as many as 100 trial cross-pollination combinations that are then extensively tested in various climates and condi-

Right: These charming snapdragons without the "snap" are not designed to conceal nectar but to appeal to the public.
Top: This exquisite orchid is from the Philippines. Orchids are more readily hybridized than many flowers, so orchid fanciers and breeders are creating new ones all the time, tailoring the traits to current fashion and whim.

tions. Only the best are selected for "experimental hybrid" status. These are further studied and weeded out until finally one choice hybrid emerges that meets all the breeder's marketing and economic criteria. Then seeds from the parent lines must be increased from small quantities so sufficient seeds can be harvested for full-scale production.

The parent plants for cross-pollination are grown indoors in controlled conditions where no insect can slip in and fertilize a plant with a rogue gene, like a mongrel dog creeping into a breeding kennel. This often takes place in developing countries with good year-round climates, such as Kenya, Chile, China and in Central American nations. To avoid "selfing," or the mixing of pollen, these hermaphrodite parent plants are assigned either a male or female role, then new female flowers are opened and the male parts are skillfully removed by hand, a process known as "emasculation." Next they are dusted with pollen from the male parts that have been selected as their partners. The process varies with each species, but it is very labor intensive and the timing is critical as the stigmas of some types of flowers are only receptive for a few hours. Petunias are hand-pollinated by workers using tiny brushes; marigolds and zinnias can be worked over with vacuum guns, and there is little chance for romance for pansies. The male parent flower is picked up and rubbed in the face of the female flower.

People love long-lasting double flowers such as this hollyhock and rose. It is difficult for insects and birds to visit the blooms, so they tend to last for a long time, waiting in vain for fertilization. Hundreds of garden and florist flowers are now produced with double blooms.

Top: Hollyhock with frilly pink petals like a ballerina's tutu
Bottom: Double rose with little room for pollinators

One of the many technological advances in the plant breeding industry is pelleting individual seeds, coating them so they look like pills in a pharmacy. The pills can be planted by hand or machine singly and accurately, saving time and money. Studies show that during seed storage the right temperature and moisture content can be critical to germination in some species. Gardeners should read seed packets carefully.

Breeders are selecting hybrids for our gardens that can be started by professionals in packs so that our small yards can have almost instant color each spring. The current trend is to grow plants that travel well and flower early. They need to be uniformly-sized, sturdy and compact. Profusely blooming plants with upward-facing, large, bold flowers are popular with consumers. Population explosions mean that people are living in ever smaller spaces, so dwarf and miniature flowering plants for pots and hanging baskets are increasingly important. New trends to look for in the future are flowering plants that are even more disease resistant, use less water and need fewer pesticides. More plants will be sexless, without pollen or untidy seeds, which is grand for people with allergies but is not so good for bees. Pollenless sunflowers are already acclaimed cut-flowers, and double-headed sunflowers that look good coming and going have been introduced. Plants that irritate our skin less, require minimum care and are color-coordinated to match special occasions in every nation are all on the drawing boards for the gardens of the next century.

While all this industrial production is taking place, mostly in Holland, England, the United States and Japan, there are countless other growers, botanic gardens and individual breeders who con-

Top: These orange-colored pocketbook flowers are planned to coordinate with Halloween decorations.
Bottom: Godetia have an ethereal beauty in the garden and as cut flowers.

tinue to work quietly on other garden plants. They constantly come up with basketfuls of new hybrids and new names. Some are great improvements, some beautiful, a few ghastly. Almost all garden plants available today are the result of special propagation, much like agricultural crops and farm animals. A few good plants are being lost, but more are being created every day. New blue roses, pink daffodils and chocolate-scented flowers fill garden catalogs annually. Other dedicated plantsmen and women are taking a renewed interest in their immediate environment, and are breeding old standbys and local wildflowers to create garden plants that are better adapted to particular climates and pollinators. Breeding of all types is an essentially creative occupation, and people have enjoyed devoting their lives to it.

Hybrid gerbera daisies have stormed garden centers on every continent in the last decade and deserve their huge success.

9 FAREWELL TO THE FAMILY

As far as plants are concerned, the whole point of sex in the garden is the successful production of seeds. Gardeners and other horticulturalists replicate their plants in all sorts of cunning ways. Copies can be made of existing plants with cuttings, grafts, by layering and by divisions. Plants can increase their numbers by themselves with root suckers and runners, bulbs, tubers, corms and rhizomes. Succulent plants called hen-and-checks probably have the quaintest system: round little offspring can roll off the parent's back to start a fresh life.

The most common way to create another plant, however, is by sexual propagation—that is by seed. Whether the seeds are from self- or cross-pollination plants, the seeds and their dispersal are as diverse and extraordinary as the plants' sexual activity. Seeds are the distributors of the plants genes and their effective dispersal is crucial to the evolution of the plant. Plants use insects as a major pollinating partner, but wind and water move most seeds around. When the weather allows, fine parachutes of fine hairs waft single seeds of some composite flowers through the air. They can close up when it rains and when the seed lands, the delicate conveyance is discarded. Seeds with papery wings, air sacs and feathery tails are blown, or float, to new locations. Countless seeds are simply picked up and thrown about in a storm.

Many seeds continue to have intimate relationships with animals, as they hitchhike on unwitting birds and mammals. Tasty seeds are eaten and dropped off in new areas. Other seeds cling with prickles, hooks or hairs to fur, feathers, beaks, hooves and muddy feet. Ideally they will be transported to a somewheat altered situation, where there is always the possibility that the new plant will do better.

There are plants who rely on their own exploding ovaries to send their genes a few feet away. Violets can throw their children out violently. Impatiens, aptly named, send their seeds flying when their sensitive pods are touched.

A flower's apparent simplicity, innocence and lack of involvement with the problems of our world are part of their appeal to gardeners. Discovering that plants advertise and compete like humans makes them more understandable, and creates a further bond between us. Learned gardeners can lead a groundswell of interest as they consider not only the plants and flowers, but also their partners and environment as a dynamic and intimately interactive system. We share with plants, among other things, the will to live, the ability to adapt and the desire to reproduce. In the next century, the questions of whose genes will be reproduced will likely propagate far beyond the quiet walls of the weekend botanist. As we consider the questions of the future, we may find some succor as close as the nearest garden. Evolving through deluge and drought, and flowering with or without pollination, plants are sublimely optimistic.

FURTHER READING

Bristow, Alec. *The Sex Life of Plants*. New York: Holt, Rhinehart and Winston, 1978.

Church, M. A., D.Sc., Arthur H. *Types of Floral Mechanism*. Part I–X11 (Jan.–April). Oxford, England: Clarendon Press, 1908.

Darwin, Charles. *The Different Forms of Flowers on Plants of the Same Species*. New York: D. Appleton and Co., 1896.

Darwin, Charles. *The Various Contrivances by Which Orchids Are Fertilized by Insects*. London, England: John Murray, 1890.

Dowden, Anne Ophelia. *From Fruit to Flower*. New York: Thomas Y. Crowell, 1984.

Dowden, Anne Ophelia. *The Clover and the Bee*. New York: Harper Collins, 1990.

Faegri, K. and Van Der Pijl, L. *The Principals of Pollination Ecology*. Oxford, England: Pergamon Press, 1971.

Heady, Eleanor B. *Plants on the Go*. New York: *Parent's* Magazine Press, 1975.

Holm, Eigil. *On Pollination and Pollinators in Western Australia*. Denmark: Eigil Holm, 1988.

Lovell, John H. *The Flower and the Bee*. New York: Charles Scribner's Sons, 1918.

Lubbock, Sir John. *British Wild Flowers in Relation to Insects*. London, England: Macmillan and Co. 1897.

McGregor, S. E. *Insect Pollination of Cultivated Crop Plants*. Washington, D.C.: U.S. Dept. of Agriculture, 1976.

Meeuse, Bastiaan, and Morris, Sean. *The Sex Life of Flowers*. New York: Facts on File Publications, 1984.

Oliver, F. W., M.A., D.Sc. *The Natural History of Plants: Their Forms, Growth and Reproduction*. From the German of Anton Kerner von Marliaun. New York: Henry Holt and Co., 1895.

Proctor, Michael, and Yeo, Peter. *The Pollination of Flowers*. New York: Taplinger Publishing Co., 1972.

Richards, A. J. *The Pollination of Flowers by Insects*. London, England: Academic Press, 1978.

Robertson, C. *Flowers and Insects*. Lancaster, P.A.: Science Press Printing Co., 1929.

Selsam, Millicent E., and Wexler, Jerome. *The Amazing Dandelion*. New York: William Morrow and Co., 1977

Van den Ende, H. *Sexual Interaction of Plants*. London, England: Acadaemic Press, 1976.

Van der Pijl, L., and Dodson, Calaway H. *Orchid Flowers, Their Pollination and Evolution*. Miami, FL.: The Fairchild Tropical Garden and the Univeristy of Miami Press, 1966.

Wilson, Mary F. *Plant Reproductive Ecology*. New York: John Wiley and Sons, 1983.

Zomlefer, Wendy B. *Flowering Plant Families*. Chapel Hill and London: The University of North Carolina Press, 1994.

INDEX

Acanthus, 69 (photo)
Adam-and-Eve, 72, 72 (photo)
Agave, 101
Alder (Alnus), 103
Alfalfa, 51
Allium, 55 (photo), 95 (photo)
Amaryllis, 63 (photo)
Anemone, 23, 23 (photo), 80
Angiosperms, 9
Annual, 17
Ant, 95
Anther, 11, 10 (drawing), 22
    disc flower, 58
    peony, 15 (photo)
Aphrodisiac, 71
Arisaemas, 72, 73, 73 (photo)
Arum, 72, 72 (photo)
Arum italicum, 72
Aster (Aster), 57, 58
Australian banksia, 100, 100 (photo)
Australian honey possum, 100 (photo)
Azalea, 83 (photo)

Banner, 50, 50 (drawing)
Bat, 38, 101
Beard tongue, 98. See also Penstemon
Bearded iris, 52 (photo), 53
Bee(s), 78. See also Bumblebee; Honeybee;
    Leaf cutter bee; Robber bee
    and cacti, 101
    color preference, 31, 37
    flower preferences, 21, 21 (photo), 48,
    49, 50, 60, 76, 77 (photo), 79 (photo)
    and natural selection of flowers, 9
    and nectar, 67, 75
    and pollen, 68, 69, 71 (photo)
    scent preference, 30, 38, 39
    and sexless plants, 110
    shape preference, 42, 44
    and shelter of flower, 70, 70 (photo)
Bee balm (Monarda didyma), 89, 99
Bee guide, 33, 33 (photo)

Bee purple, 31
Beech (Fagus), 102, 103
Beetle, 9, 9 (photo)
    breeding on flower, 71 (photo)
    flower preference, 94
    and pollen, 68
    scent preference, 38
Begonia, 21, 21 (photo), 69
Bellflower, 25 (photo)
Bell-shaped flower, 42
Bird-of-paradise (Strelitzia reginae), 100
Birds, 96–99
    and butterfly, 88
    and cacti, 101
    and flower pollination, 8, 54, 55, 71,
    100, 103
    and nectar, 66
Bisexual flowers, 22–23
Blazing star (Liatris punctata sp.), 56, 56
    (photo), 58, 90
Blue bonnet (Lupinus texensis), 37
Blue chicory (Chicorium intybus), 61
Blue mist spirea, 71 (photo)
Bougainvillea, 18, 18 (photo), 99
Bowl-shaped flower(s), 9, 40 (drawing), 41,
    41 (photo)
    similarity among, 63
Bract, 18, 18 (photo)
Breeding site, 71
Broadbill hummingbird, 97 (photo)
Broom (flower), 51 (photo)
Bulb, 17, 112
Bumblebee, 25 (photo), 42, 84 (photo). See
    also Bee; Honeybee; Leaf cutter bee; Rob-
    ber bee
    flower preference, 42, 54, 82–83
    and monkshood, 25 (photo), 51
Buttercup (Ranunculus), 25, 63, 67
Butterfly, 9, 86–89
    color preference, 31
    flower preferences, 86, 86 (photo), 87
    (photo), 89

Butterfly (continued)
    and moth, difference between, 90
    and nectar, 67, 75, 75 (photo)
    scent preference, 38, 89
    shape preference, 42, 44
    size of flowers, 54, 55
Butterfly bush (Buddleia), 55, 89
Butterfly flower (Asclepias tuberosa), 75, 75
    (photo)

Cactus, 97 (photo), 101
California fuchsia (Zauschneria californica),
    14, 98
California poppy (Eschscholzia californica),
    41 (photo), 62
Camellia, 69
Camouflage, 71, 71 (photo), 88, 88 (photo)
Campanulas, 11, 58, 82
Cape honeysuckle (Tecomaria capensis), 98
Cape primrose, 33
Cardinal climber (Ipomoea quamoclit), 99
Cardinal flower (Lobelia cardinalis), 99
Cardoon cactus, 101
Carpel, 14
Carrion-eating fly, 31, 38
Carrot (Daucus carota), 67
Carrot family (Umbelliferae), 55
Catkins, 103 (photo)
Checkered lily, 60 (photo)
Chemical barriers, 23
Cherry laurel (Prunus laureocerasus), 95
Chestnut tree, 105 (photo)
Chiming bells, 37 (photo)
Chinese hibiscus, 99
Christmas rose (Helleborus niger), 67
Chrysanthemum (Chrysanthemum), 57
Cineraria, 20 (photo)
Cinquefoil (Potentilla), 63
Clary sage, 82 (photo)
Claw (flower), 100 (photo)
Clematis, 69, 70 (photo)
Cleome, 55 (photo)

Colchicum autumnale, 62, 62 (photo)
Color of flowers, 30–32, 30 (photo)
    and butterfly, 86, 89
    change after pollination, 37, 37 (photo)
    and fly, 92, 93
    hairs on flower, 53, 53 (photo)
    and honeybee, 81 (photo)
    how produced, 32
    and hummingbird, 96, 97–99
Columbine, 19, 19 (photo), 98 (photo)
Column, 56
Composite flowers, 57, 57 (photo), 58, 58
    (photo), 59, 59 (photo)
Cone-bearing plants, ancient, 9
Coneflower, 45 (photo), 57
Conifer, 102
Copycat plants, 63
Coral bells (Heuchera), 99
Coriander, 55
Corm, 112
Cornflower (Centaurea cyanus), 57
Cosmos (Cosmos), 57, 58, 59
Cottonwood, 24
Crab spider, 71
Crambe, 93 (photo)
Crocus, 14, 60 (photo)
Cross-pollination, 20, 25, 64
    and finch, 100
    and hummingbird, 99
    plant-breeding industry, 107–9
    by wind, 102
Crown imperial, 66
Cumin, 55
Cupid's dart (Catananche caerulea), 59
Cutting, 112
Cyclamen, 107

Daffodil, 42, 42 (photo)
Dahlia (Dahlia), 57, 81 (photo)
Daisy (Bellis), 25
    composite/ray flower, 57, 57 (photo), 59
    gerbera daisy, 111 (photo)
    pollen grain, 12 (drawing)
    white daisy, 31, 59
Dame's rocket, 55 (photo)
Dandelion, 25 (photo), 67

Date tree, 24
Datura, 14, 61
Daylily, 34 (photo), 62
Dead head, 17
Delivery and receptive system, 51
Delphinium, 44, 48, 48 (drawing), 53, 53
    (photo)
    red delphinium (Delphinium cardinale), 98
Dianthus, cover, 107
Dill, 55
Disc flower, 58, 58 (photo)
Division, 112
Dogwood, 18, 93 (photo)
Donkey tail spurge (Euphorbia myrsinites), 67,
    67 (photo)
Double rose, 109 (photo)
Drone (bee), 78
Dutchman's pipe, 23

Egg. See Ovule
Elderberry (Sambucus), 94
Elephant's ear plant (Alocasia sp.), 74, 74
    (photo)
Eucera bee, 77 (photo)
Evening primrose (Oenothera), 22, 39, 90,
    90 (photo)

F1 hybrids, 107
Fall flowers, 62, 62 (photo)
False indigo (Baptisia), 50, 50 (drawing)
Female reproductive organs, 7, 9, 10 (draw-
    ing), 14–19
Ferns, 9
Figwort, 51
Filament, 10 (drawing), 11, 58
Finch, 100
Fireweed, 22
Flaming trumpet (Pyrostegia venusta), 98
Flowering dogwood, 18, 93 (photo)
Fly, 92–93
    carrion-eating, 31, 38
    color preference, 31
    flower preference, 92–93
    and lords-and-ladies, 72
    on orchid, 77 (photo)
    and pollen, 68

Fly (continued)
    scent preference, 38, 73, 73 (photo)
    syrphid fly, 67
Forget-me-not (Myositis), 93
Forsythia, 60 (photo)
Four-o'clock (Mirabilis jalapa), 61
Foxglove, 33, 42, 42 (photo)
    and bumblebee, 82
    Greek foxglove, 44 (photo)
Foxtail lily, 56 (photo)
Fruit trees, 67
Fuchsia, 10 (drawing), 11, 14, 99
    California fuchsia (Zauschneria
    californica), 98

Gardenia, 39
Gentian, 17 (photo)
Geraniums (Pelargoniums), 11, 107
Gerbera daisy, 111
Gladiolus, 56 (photo)
Gloxinia, 32, 32 (photo)
Gnat, 73
Godetia, 110 (photo)
Gold finch, 98 (photo)
Goldsmith Seeds, 107
Good-luck plant (Oxalis), 93
Graft, 112
Grape (Vitis sp.), 67
Grasses, 102, 103, 103 (photo)
Greek foxglove (Digitalis lanata), 44 (photo)
Green pea pod, 16
Gymnosperms, 9

Hairy flowers, 52–53, 52 (photo)
Hare bell, 58
Heliotrope, 39, 39 (photo)
Hellebores, 23 (photo)
Helleborine (Epipactis), 85
Hen-and-chick, 112
Hermaphrodites, 103, 109
Hibiscus, 13 (photo), 14
    Chinese hibiscus (Hibiscus rosa-sinensis),
    99
Himalayan border jewel (Polygonum affine),
    104, 104 (photo)
Holly, 21, 21 (photo)

Hollyhock, 109 (photo)
Honey comb, 80
Honey guide. *See* Bee guide
Honeybee *(Apis mellifera)*, 71–81. *See also*
   Bee; Bumblebee; Leaf cutter bee; Robber
   bee
   color preference, 31 (drawing)
   and nectar, 66
   and pollen, 68–69, 68 (photo)
   and propolis, 71
   and scent, 38
   shape preference, 42
Honeysuckle *(Lonicera)*, 67 (photo)
   bisexual, 22
   and hummingbird, 98
   and moth, 90
   stigma placement, 14
Human fetus, 16 (photo)
Hummingbird, 19
   broadbill hummingbird, 97 (photo)
   color preference, 31, 31 (drawing), 96–
   99
   flower preferences, 96 (photo), 97–99
   and nectar, 66, 100
   shape preference, 42
Hyacinth, 38, 56
Hybrid plants, 107, 110
Hydrangeas, 32
Hyssops *(Agastache)*, 89

Ice plant *(Delosperma* sp.), 61
Iceland poppy, 93 (photo)
Impatiens, 89, 107, 113
Inflorescence, 55, 89
Insects, 8, 103
   camouflaged on flower, 71, 71 (photo)
   flower preferences, 41, 54, 55, 57, 70,
   74
   and nectar, 66
   and pollen, 68
Inula *(Inula)*, 57
Iris, 53, 81 (photo)

Jack-in-the-pulpit *(Arisaema triphyllum)*, 24,
   72, 73, 73 (photo)
Jewelweed *(Impatiens capensis)*, 62, 98

Jimsonweed *(Datura stramonium)*, 90
Juniper *(Juniperus)*, 103

Keel (petals), 50, 50 (drawing)
Kentucky coffee tree, 24
Knapweed, 57

Ladies' teardrops *(Fuchsia)*, 99
Landing platform, 40 (drawing)
Larkspur, 56
Laurel, 66
Lavender, 38, 39
Layering, 112
Leaf cutter bee, 83. *See also* Bee; Bumble-
   bee; Honeybee; Robber bee
Lesser periwinkle *(Vinca minor)*, 93
Lilac *(Syringa)*, 39, 55
Lily, 11, 14, 33, 34 (photo), 42 (photo)
   checkered lily, 60 (photo)
   foxtail lily, 56 (photo)
   crown imperial, 66
   length of availability to pollinator, 62
   water lily, 75
Lily-of-the-valley, 38
Linden *(Tilia)*, 104
Lords-and-Ladies *(Arum maculatum)*, 72, 72
   (photo)
Lungwort *(Pulmonaria)*, 93
Lupine *(Lupinus)*, 50, 50 (photo)

Magnolia, 9 (photo), 23
Male reproductive organs, 7, 9, 10 (draw-
   ing), 11
Maltese cross, 88 (photo)
Malva, 29 (photo)
Mammals
   and flowers, 8, 54
   and nectar, 66
Maple tree, 102
Marigold, 83 (photo)
   plant-breeding industry, 107, 109
   pot marigold *(Calendula)*, 89
Meadow rue *(Thalictrum)*, 104, 104 (photo)
Mexican sunflower *(Tithonia)*, 84 (photo), 89
Mice, 39
Mint *(Mentha)*, 22, 22 (photo), 51, 89

Monkshood *(Aconitum* sp.), 25, 25 (photo),
   51
Montbretia *(Crocosmia)*, 97 (photo), 98
Morning glory, 33
Moss rose, 41 (photo)
Moth, 90
   flower preferences, 54, 89, 90 (photo)
   hummingbird hawkmoth, 91, 91 (photo)
   and natural selection, 9
   scent preference, 38
   Sphinx moth, 39
Mountain laurel *(Kalmia latifolia)*, 51
Mouse plant *(Arisarum proboscideum)*, 73,
   73 (photo)
Mullein, 56 (photo), 68
Mustard *(Brassicaceae)*, 67
Mutation, 20

Narcissus, paper-white, 38
Nasturtium *(Tropaeolum)*, 19, 19 (photo), 66,
   98
   and hummingbird hawkmoth, 91, 91
   (photo)
Natural selection, 9, 21
Nectar, 66–67
   and ant, 95
   and bat, 101
   and beetle, 94
   and butterfly, 86
   and flies, 92 (photo), 93
   and hummingbird, 96, 99, 100
   and wasp, 85
Nectar guide. *See* Bee guide
Nectaroscordum siculum, 85 (photo)
Nectary, 10 (drawing), 19, 66
   butterfly flower, 75, 75 (photo)
New Holland honey eater, 100 (photo)
"Niche marketing," 60

Oak tree *(Quercus)*, 102, 103
Obedient plant *(Physotegia)*, 62
Oleander, 28 (photo)
Oncidium henekenii orchid, 76, 77 (photo)
Ophrys fuciflora orchid, 76, 77 (photo)
Optimism of plants, 113

Orchid
    as breeding site, 71
    and color, 37
    hybrids, 108 (photo),
    length of availability to pollinator, 62
    oncidium henekenii orchid, 77 (photo)
    ophrys fuciflora orchid, 77 (photo)
    pollinators, specific, 51
    pseudo-copulation, 76
    scent, 39
    stamens, 11
    Trichoceros antennifera orchid, 77 (photo)
Organ pipe cactus, 101
Oriental poppy, 32 (photo)
Oswego tea *(Monarda didyma)*, 99
Ovary, 9, 10 (drawing), 14, 16. *See also*
    Ovule
    disc flower, 58
    gentian, 17 (photo)
    peony, 15 (photo)
    poppy, 17 (photo)
Ovule, 10 (drawing), 16, 17. *See also* Ovary
    disc flower, 58

Pansy, 32, 32 (photo)
    plant-breeding industry, 107, 109
Paper-white narcissus, 38
Pasque flower, 23, 53 (photo)
Pea, 50, 51, 52, 52 (photo)
Pear *(Pyrus)*, 67
Pearly everlasting *(Anaphalis)*, 58
Pelleting of seeds, 110
Penstemon, 11, 22, 53 (photo), 68, 81
    (photo), 99 (photo)
    beard tongue *(Penstemon barbatus* and
        Penstemon eatonii), 98
    and bumblebee, 82
    dusky penstemon, 85 (photo)
Peony, 15 (photo), 41
Pepper seeds, 16 (photo)
Perennial, 17
Peruvian lily *(Alstroemeria)*, 22 (photo)
Petal, 18, 18 (photo)
Petunia, 14, 107, 109
Phlox, 42, 89
Pine *(Picus)*, 9, 102, 103

Pin-eyed primrose, 24, 24 (drawing)
Pink (flower), 44 (photo)
Pistil, 10 (drawing), 14, 22
    disc flower, 58
Pitcher plant *(Sarracenia* sp.), 74, 74 (photo)
Plant-breeding industry, 106–11
Plum *(Prunus)*, 67
Pocketbook flower, 110 (photo)
Poinsettia, 18
Pollen, 10 (drawing), 11, 12, 12 (drawing),
    68–69
    and ultraviolet light damage, 105
    and wind pollination, 102
Pollen tube, 10 (drawing), 15
Pollination by humans. *See* Seed industry
Pollinators, 8, 11. *See also* individual polli-
    nator names
    attracting, 26–63
Poplar *(Populus)*, 103
Poppy *(Papaver)*, 1, 32
    bee flower, 69, 80
    California   poppy   *(Eschscholzia
        californica)*, 41 (photo), 62
    Iceland poppy, 93 (photo)
    length of availability, 62
    Oriental poppy, 32 (photo)
Possum, 100
    Australian honey possum, 100 (photo)
Pot marigold *(Calendula)*, 89
Potato *(Solanum)*, 94
Prickly pear, 71 (photo)
Primrose *(Primula vulgaris)*, 24, 24 (drawing),
    31
    Cape primrose, 33 (photo)
    evening primrose, 22, 39
    fly flower, 93
    plant-breeding industry, 107
Propolis, 71
Pseudo-copulation, 76
Pussytoes *(Antennaria)*, 58

Queen Anne's lace, 55
Queen bee, 78, 80, 82

Raspberry *(Rubus)*, 67
Ray flower, 59, 59 (photo)

Red columbine *(Aquilegia canadensis)*, 98
Red delphinium *(Delphinium cardinale)*, 98
Red fairy trumpet *(Ipomopsis aggregata)*, 42
Red-hot-poker *(Kniphfia uvaria)*, 37 (photo),
    98, 98 (photo), 100
Reproductive organs, 7, 9, 10–19
Rhizome, 112
Rhododendron, 69
Robber bee, 83. *See also* Bee; Bumblebee;
    Honeybee; Leaf cutter bee
Robin's nest, 17 (photo)
Rock-foil *(Saxifraga* sp.), 67
Root sucker, 112
Rose *(Rosa)*, 11, 23, 39 (photo)
    bee flower, 69, 69 (photo), 80, 83
    beetle flower, 94
    color, 30
    double rose, 109 (photo)
    moss rose, 41 (photo)
    scent, 38, 39
    shape, 41, 41 (photo)
    sun rose, 68 (photo)
Rose Mallow, 94
Runner, 112
Rushes, 103, 104

Sage *(Artemisia)*, 56, 58
Sage *(Salvia guaranitica, Salvia elegans,*
    Salvia greggii), 98
Saguaro cactus, 101
Salvia, 56
Scarlet gilia *(Ipomopsis aggregata)*, 98
Scarlet monkey flower *(Mimulus cardinalis)*,
    99
Scent as pollinator attraction, 30, 33, 38–
    39
    and bat, 101
    change after pollination, 37
    elephant's ear plant, 74
    mouse plant, 73, 73 (photo)
Sea lavender *(Limonium)*, 93
Seed(s), 9, 112–13
Seed dispersal, 112–13
Seed head, 103 (photo)
Seed industry, 51, 106–11
Segregated sexes, 24

Self-fertilization. *See* Selfing
Selfing, 20, 21, 22, 23, 25
Self-pollination. *See* Selfing
Sepal, 18, 18 (photo)
"Series" of plants, 107–8
Sex determination, 24
Sex organs. *See* Reproductive organs
Sexual orientation of flowers, 20–25
    bisexual, 22–23
    segregated sexes, 24
    selfing, 25
Shape of flower, 9, 40–45, 86, 89
Shelter, flowers as, 70
Shrimp plant *(Justicia brandegeana)*, 99
Shrub, 102
Size of flowers, 54–55, 54 (photo), 55 (photo)
Slug, 8, 74
Snail, 74
Snakeweed *(Polygonum bistorta)*, 104
Snapdragon, 49, 49 (photo), 107, 108
    (photo)
Snowdrop *(Galanthus)*, 67
Snow-in-summer, 93 (photo)
South African protea, 39, 100
Spadix, 72
Spanish bayonet *(Yucca)*, 37
Sphinx moth, 39
Spider, 71, 85
Spore-bearing plants, ancient, 9
Sprekelia, 21 (photo)
Spring flowers, 60, 60 (photo)
Spruce *(Picea)*, 103
Squash, 21, 21 (photo)
Stamen, 10 (drawing), 11, 11 (drawing), 22
    wind-pollinated plant, 103
Stem, 58

Stigma, 10 (drawing), 14, 15, 22
    disc flower, 58, 58 (photo)
    wind-pollinated plant, 103
St.-John's-wort *(Hypericum)*, 69
Strawberry *(Fragaria)*, 67
Style, 10 (drawing), 15, 58
Summer flowers, 61, 61 (photo), 87 (photo)
Sun rose *(Helianthemum* sp.), 23, 63, 68
    (photo)
Sundew *(Drosera)*, 74
Sunflower *(Helianthus)*, 57
    Mexican sunflower *(Tithonia)*, 84 (photo),
    89
    pollenless, 110
Swallowtail butterfly, 87 (photo)
Sweet pea *(Lathyrus odoratus)*, 50
Syrphid flies, 67

Tactile aids as pollinator attraction, 33, 34
    (photo), 53, 53 (photo)
Tepal, 18, 18 (photo)
Thistle, 57
Thorn apple *(Datura)*, 14, 61
Thrum-eyed primrose, 24, 24 (drawing)
Thyme *(Thymus)*, 93
Tibouchina, 68
Tickseed *(Bidens aristosa)*, 89
Tobacco flower *(Nicotiana* sp.), 39, 89, 90
Trailing lantana *(Lantana montevidensis)*, 88,
    99
Tree fern, 9 (photo)
Trees, 102–3
"True" plant populations, 107
Trumpet honeysuckle *(Lonicera sempervirens)*,
    98
Trumpet vine *(Campsis radicans)*, 98

Trumpet-shaped flower, 42–43
Tuber, 112
Tulip, 18, 18 (photo)

Venus's flytrap *(Dionaea muscipula)*, 74
Verbena *(Verbena* sp.), 34 (photo), 37
    (photo), 89, 89 (photo)
Vetch *(Vicia)*, 95
Viburnum, 39 (photo)
Violet, 14, 25, 38
Viper's bugloss, 36 (photo)
Visual aids as pollinator attraction, 33

Wallflower, 36 (photo)
Walnut tree *(Juglans)*, 103
Wasp, 38, 51, 76, 85
Water Lily *(Nymphaea)*, 23, 75, 75 (photo)
Water birch *(Betula occidentalis)*, 103 (photo)
White daisy, 59
Wild ginger *(Asarum canadense)*, 92
Wildflower, 82
Willow *(Salix)*, 104, 104 (photo)
Wind pollination, 102–5
    with insect pollination, 104
Windflower, 60 (photo), 63
Wine cup *(Callirhoe involucrata)*, 37
Wings (petals), 50, 50 (drawing)

Yarrow *(Achillea)*, 45 (photo), 57, 94 (photo)
Yew *(Taxus)*, 103

Zinnia *(Zinnia)*, 57, 89
    plant-breeding industry, 107, 109

A Bouquet of Thanks—

Not much happens in a vacuum, least of all sex and books. I am indebted to, and would like to thank all the friends, family members and colleagues who provided me with knowledge, help and encouragement. Some should have their name in lights, others provided smaller bits of crucial help just when I needed it. The alphabetized list includes: Sybil Bashor, Alexandra Elliott, Goldsmith Seeds, Evelyn Kaye, Ellice Keyes, Tweet Kimball, David Macke, Margaret Maupin, Marjorie McIntosh, David Miltz, Shirley Nelson, Charles Overy, Belinda Platts, Peta Poore, Rob Proctor, Beckie Smith, Lauren Springer, Linda Staley, Jeanne Stanwood, John Stone, Nancy Styler, Marcia Tatroe, Bryan Wright (a model with Next Agency, Vienna, Austria), and two very kind women who let me photograph them at the train station in Richmond. Many thanks to the artists and photographers who contibuted gorgeous pictures, and to the kind people on four continents who let me photograph their gardens.
I am grateful to everyone at the Denver Botanic Gardens, especially Panayoti Kelaidis, Paula Ogilvie, Joe Tomocik and Susan Eubank. Finally a floral tribute to Fulcrum Publishing, particularly Charlotte and Robert Baron, and Jay Staten. They are a joy to work with.
Every author should be lucky enough to have Fulcrum publish their book.